Journeys through God's Word

An Introductory Course:

PSALMS

Study Guide

Steven Mueller

CPH
SAINT LOUIS

Edited by Thomas J. Doyle

This publication is available in braille and in large print for the visually impaired. Write to the Library for the Blind, 1333 S. Kirkwood Rd., St. Louis, MO 63122-7295; or call 1-800-433-3954.

Copyright © 1998 Concordia Publishing House
3558 South Jefferson Avenue, St. Louis, MO 63118-3968
Manufactured in the United States of America

1   2   3   4   5   6   7   8   9 10   08   07   06   05   04   03   02   01   00   99

Contents

Introduction

The study of the Bible is nothing less than an exploration into the thoughts and desires of God for ordinary people like you and me. It takes us from this hardened and selfish world into the promise of a world where God's peace, justice, and mercy will be complete.

Delving into the Bible for the first time can be somewhat intimidating. We are taken to a distant past that is full of unfamiliar customs and traditions. We must become acquainted with a nation that viewed the world differently than many people do today. And we must begin to alter some of our current definitions to grasp the full meaning of our Lord's love and compassion.

As foreign as many customs and traditions might seem to us today, we will discover that people's natures remain the same. We are trapped today—as people were centuries ago—in an imperfect world where evil and pain seem all too prevalent. We, too, can view the world as meaningless and without hope. But Jesus Christ came to rescue the world from its quagmire, and His deliverance continues to change our life. Pray that the Word of God will begin to alter your perspective. May His promises give you rich and lasting hope and joy!

How to Use This Study

The Study Guide will direct your study of Psalms. The typical session is divided into five parts:

1. Approaching This Study
2. An Overview
3. Working with the Text
4. Applying the Message
5. Taking the Message Home

"Approaching This Study" is intended to whet the reader's appetite for the topics at hand. It leads participants into the world of the Old Testament while summarizing the issues to be examined. "An Overview" summarizes the textual material used in each session. Before the text is examined in detail, it is viewed as a whole, allowing participants to "see the forest" before "exploring the trees." "Working with the Text" draws participants into deeper biblical study, encouraging them to discover the gems of universal truth that lie in the details of God's Word. When questions appear difficult or unclear, the Leader Guide provides a doorway to the answers. "Applying the Message" leads participants from the recorded Word of God to its possible application in our present lives. It helps participants more fully realize the implications of God's Word for their daily experience as a Christian. Finally, "Taking the Message Home" invites participants to continue their scriptural meditation at home. Suggestions are given for personal reflection, for preview of the following session, and for private study of topics raised by the session. The study of God's Word will be greatly enhanced by those actively pursuing the suggestions offered in this section.

Each session ends with some trivia that is intended to spark interest and generate additional discussion. This can be used to develop inquisitiveness and enthusiasm about related issues that are ripe for exploration.

A glossary is provided at the end of the Study Guide. Because a study of the Bible will lead participants to language that may occasionally seem foreign and difficult, the glossary will make participants more comfortable with unfamiliar terms, phrases, and customs. The glossary will help them understand biblical concepts such as love and grace, whose definitions may differ from current definitions.

Session 1

How to Read the Psalms: Be in the Covenant

Psalm 1

Approaching This Study

"Cheaters never prosper," says the old proverb. But it's not hard for us to think of many times when this isn't true. We know of many situations when cheaters do prosper and the "nice guys finish last." We wish the world was so simple that those who do good were rewarded and those who do evil were always punished. But life on this earth is not so simple.

These experiences might make us suspicious of the words of Psalm 1. It boldly notes the differences between the way of the righteous—those made right with God through faith in Jesus—and the way of the wicked—those who do not possess saving faith. We might be inclined to ignore the psalm and say it is too simplistic. But when we see it in context, its proclamation of God's truth shines through.

Psalm 1, along with the second psalm, serves as an introduction to the entire book and teaches us essential truths necessary if we want to understand the psalms. Psalm 1 reminds us that to understand the psalms, we must be among the righteous. However, an honest self-appraisal of our own life tells us that we are often in the way of the wicked. But God has made us righteous people through our faith in Christ Jesus—we are people who not only understand the psalms, but apply the truths they teach to our life.

An Overview

Psalms are written in a poetic form and are designed for use as songs in worship. Psalm 1, which serves as an introduction to the entire psalter, teaches that understanding the psalms requires a faith relationship with

God. God alone provides understanding. Psalm 1 can be divided into three basic sections:

The Way of the Righteous (verses 1–3)

The Way of the Wicked (verses 4–5)

Conclusion (verse 6)

Working with the Text

Hebrew Poetry

1. Psalms is a book of poetry. However, Hebrew poetry may not seem like poetry to a modern English reader. These poems do not rhyme—either in English or in Hebrew. There is little sense of rhythm to them when translated. Two things distinguish Hebrew poetry from prose. First, Hebrew poetry uses very descriptive language, filled with metaphors and vivid comparisons. For example, Psalm 23:1 begins "The LORD is my shepherd." The words are familiar to us, but the language is metaphorical. Through this metaphor, the psalmist reveals the amazing care that God provides. What other examples of descriptive language in the psalms or the rest of the Bible can you think of?

2. A second major characteristic of Hebrew poetry is parallelism. An idea may be stated several times, each time in a different, more intense manner. Psalm 51:2 is a good example of parallelism. How does the parallel emphasize the point?

Wash away all my iniquity
and cleanse me from my sin. (Psalm 51:2)

Another example is found in the opening verses of Psalm 96. How does the writer expand the idea with each repetition?

Sing to the LORD a new song;
sing to the LORD, all the earth.
Sing to the LORD, praise His name.
(Psalm 96:1–2a)

Another example of Hebrew poetry is usually spoken at the end of the divine service. The pastor blesses the congregation with the words of Numbers 6:24–26. What does this parallel suggest to you about the nature of God?

The LORD bless you and keep you;

the LORD make His face shine upon you and be gracious to you;

the LORD turn His face toward you and give you peace.

(Numbers 6:24–26)

As you read the psalms, watch for the richness of images and parallels.

The Psalms and Music

Remember that psalms were written to be sung. The psalter is a hymnal. Many of the psalms begin with an ascription giving specific information. Psalm 5, for example, is prefaced with the words "For the director of music. For flutes. A psalm of David."

Not only does this tell us the author (one of 73 psalms ascribed to David), but it also reminds us that the psalm is a song and directs what instruments should be used. Some of the psalms are even more specific, providing the name of the tune that the author has in mind. So Psalm 22 comes with these words: "For the director of music. To the tune of 'The Doe of the Morning.' A psalm of David."

While we don't know the specific tunes first used with these psalms, we do know that the psalms have been repeatedly set to music throughout the centuries and are still being set to new music today.

The Way of the Righteous (verses 1–3)

1. Read Psalm 1:1–3. Verse 1 defines the righteous person by things they avoid. This is a good example of parallelism. With each repetition, the psalmist compares wickedness to three actions—walking, standing, and sitting. Describe the wickedness he associates with each action. How does each action get progressively worse?

2. Describe the pattern of a righteous life (verse 2). How do Joshua 1:8 and Deuteronomy 6:6–9 amplify this point? At what times of our life are we to focus on God's Word?

> Do not let this Book of the Law depart from your mouth; meditate on it day and night, so that you may be careful to do everything written in it. Then you will be prosperous and successful. (Joshua 1:8)

> These commandments that I give you today are to be upon your hearts. Impress them on your children. Talk about them when you sit at home and when you walk along the road, when you lie down and when you get up. Tie them as symbols on your hands and bind them on your foreheads. Write them on the doorframes of your houses and on your gates. (Deuteronomy 6:6–9)

3. The psalmist describes the righteous as "blessed." The word applies to many areas of life and is often translated "oh, how happy." Jesus uses similar language in the Sermon on the Mount (Matthew 5:3–12). For example, in Matthew 5:7 Jesus teaches, "Blessed are the merciful, for they will be shown mercy." This psalm certainly implies that God will bless the person who does the things mentioned in verse 2. How might these things result in a happy life?

4. We might be tempted to quickly identify ourselves as the righteous (and therefore the blessed). What words or phrases in these verses indicate that we are unable to live a righteous life by our own power?

5. Verse 3 explains verses 1 and 2 by comparing the righteous person to a productive tree. Why does this tree do so well? See also Jeremiah 17:7–8 and John 15:5.

> But blessed is the man who trusts in the LORD, whose confidence is in Him.
> He will be like a tree planted by the water that sends out its roots by the stream.
> It does not fear when heat comes; its leaves are always green.
> It has no worries in a year of drought and never fails to bear fruit. (Jeremiah 17:7–8)

> I am the vine; you are the branches. If a man remains in Me and I in him, he will bear much fruit; apart from Me you can do nothing. (John 15:5)

The Way of the Wicked (verses 4–5)

1. Read Psalm 1:4–5. The psalmist now turns his attention to the wicked. In verse 4 he describes them as chaff. In biblical times, the production of grain was very time-consuming. After cutting the stalks of wheat, workers would beat them to separate the grain from the rest of the plant (the chaff). Once this was done, they would separate the wheat from the chaff by flinging both into the air. The grain was heavy and

would fall back to the ground, while the chaff was carried away by the wind. Contrast this description of the wicked with the depiction of the righteous found in verse 3. What are the differences, according to the psalmist?

2. Verse 1 says that the righteous do not stand in the way of sinners. According to verse 5, where will the wicked and the sinners not stand? What does this mean?

Conclusion (verse 6)

1. Read verse 6. This verse offers a summary and conclusion to the psalm. Compare the way of the righteous and the way of the wicked.

2. "The LORD watches over the way of the righteous" might more literally be translated "the Lord *knows* the way of the righteous." In Hebrew, this word—*knows*—indicates the deepest, most intimate form of knowledge. In what way does the Lord know us as righteous?

Applying the Message

1. Many people would read this psalm and interpret it to say that good people always prosper (vv. 1–3) and wicked people always fail (vv. 4–5). Does your experience indicate that this is true? Does the Bible indicate that this is true? See Matthew 5:11–12 and Luke 9:23.

Blessed are you when people insult you, persecute you and falsely say all kinds of evil against you because of Me. Rejoice and be glad, because great is your reward in heaven, for in the same way they persecuted the prophets who were before you. (Matthew 5:11–12)

If anyone would come after Me, he must deny himself and take up his cross daily and follow Me. (Luke 9:23)

2. The psalm says that the righteous man will be blessed and that the way of the wicked will perish. We might hope to be counted among the righteous, but what does God say about our righteousness in Romans 3:10–12 and Isaiah 64:6?

There is no one righteous, not even one; there is no one who understands, no who seeks God. All have turned away, they have together become worthless; there is no one who does good, not even one. (Romans 3:10–12)

All of us have become like one who is unclean, and all our righteous acts are like filthy rags; we all shrivel up like a leaf, and like the wind our sins sweep us away. (Isaiah 64:6)

3. How then can we see Psalm 1 as good news for us? See Romans 3:21–24 and Galatians 3:11.

But now a righteousness from God, apart from law, has been made known, to which the Law and the Prophets testify. This righteousness from God comes through faith in Jesus Christ to all who believe. There is no difference, for all have sinned and fall short of the glory of God, and are justified freely by His grace through the redemption that came by Christ Jesus. (Romans 3:21–24)

Clearly no one is justified before God by the law, because, "The righteous will live by faith." (Galatians 3:11)

4. Psalm 1 serves as an introduction to the entire Book of Psalms. Understanding Psalm 1 is essential for understanding all the other psalms. What do you think Psalm 1 teaches that will help us understand the rest of the psalms?

Taking the Message Home

Review

Read Psalm 1 again. How does this psalm qualify as poetry? Notice the author's use of imagery and parallelism. Also read John 15:1–8 and Romans 3:9–21. Contemplate the wonder revealed in these passages. Though we truly *"walk in the counsel of the wicked ... stand in the way of sinners [and] sit in the seat of mockers"* (Psalm 1:1), God nonetheless forgives us for Christ's sake. He "plant[s] [us] by streams of water" (Psalm 1:3), causing us to prosper as He continually watches over us.

Looking Ahead

Psalm 1 served as an introduction to the psalter. Psalm 2, which we will consider in the next session, provides another essential key for understanding the psalms: if we want to understand them, we must know Christ.

Working Ahead

1. Read Psalm 2. You may want to read it from a number of different translations.

2. During the week, consider how our world and society react to God and to His followers. Are they accepted and welcomed by the world?

Are they treated with suspicion? Are they rejected? Look for concrete examples. Why do you think society reacts this way?

Did You Know?

The Book of Psalms contains 150 different psalms. These are divided into five distinct sections or "books." They are

1. Psalm 1–41

2. Psalm 42–72

3. Psalm 73–89

4. Psalm 90–106

5. Psalm 107–150

The first four sections each end with a blessing (Psalm 41:13; 72:19; 89:52; 106:48). The fifth section doesn't end with a blessing, but Psalm 150 serves as a concluding song of praise to the entire Book of Psalms, ending *"Let everything that has breath praise the LORD. Praise the LORD."* Most scholars think that this five-fold division of the psalter is meant to correspond to the five books of Moses or Torah (the first five books of the Bible: Genesis, Exodus, Leviticus, Numbers, and Deuteronomy).

Session 2

How to Read the Psalms: Know Christ

Psalm 2

Approaching This Study

Psalm 2 is a royal psalm that describes the establishment and coronation of a king. While God established and upholds the king, the surrounding countries do not approve of the king and plan rebellion. This scenario was repeated a number of times during Israel's history. This psalm makes it clear that rebelling against the king whom God establishes is rebellion against God Himself. The psalm calls the people to submit to the king and thus to God.

While this psalm probably refers initially to an earthly king, it also points to Jesus the Messiah, a descendent of King David who will rule on David's throne forever. Israelite kings were God's children, but the Messiah is truly God's Son. Because of its clear prophecies, the New Testament quotes Psalm 2 more often than any other psalm. We understand this psalm most clearly when we see Christ in it. That is true of the entire psalter. Understanding comes from knowing Christ.

The psalm itself does not give us any background information, including the authorship. In Acts 4:25, Peter and John ascribe this psalm to David, though they may have followed a common Jewish practice of calling David the author of the entire psalter.

An Overview

This royal and messianic psalm can be divided into these sections:

The Rebellion of the Nations (verses 1–3)

The Lord's Response—a King (verses 4–6)

The King's Proclamation (verses 7–9)

To the Nations: A Warning and Blessing (verses 10–12)

Working with the Text

The Rebellion of the Nations (verses 1–3)

1. Read verses 1–3. These verses contain four sets of poetic parallels. What are they? How does the parallelism emphasize the message of these verses?

2. This section begins with a question: Why do the nations do these things? So shocked is the psalmist by people's behavior that we might better translate his question "How can they … ?" or even "Who do they think they are?" Why is this particular rebellion so shocking?

3. Verse 2 says that their rebellion is against the Lord and His Anointed One. What is the meaning of anointing? What or who is anointed in the following passages?

Anoint the Tent of Meeting, the ark of the Testimony, the table and all its articles, the lampstand and its accessories, the altar of incense, the altar of burnt offering and all its utensils, and the basin with its stand. You shall consecrate them so they will be most holy, and whatever touches them will be holy. (Exodus 30:26–29)

Then the men of Judah came to Hebron and there they anointed David king over the house of Judah. (2 Samuel 2:4)

After you put these clothes on your brother Aaron and his sons, anoint and ordain them. Consecrate them so they may serve Me as priests. (Exodus 28:41)

[Jesus] went to Nazareth, where He had been brought up, and on the Sabbath day He went into the synagogue, as was His custom.

17

And He stood up to read. The scroll of the prophet Isaiah was handed to Him. Unrolling it, He found the place where it is written:

"The Spirit of the Lord is on Me,
because He has anointed Me
to preach good news to the poor.
He has sent Me to proclaim freedom for the prisoners
and recovery of sight for the blind,
to release the oppressed,
to proclaim the year of the Lord's favor."

Then He rolled up the scroll, gave it back to the attendant and sat down. The eyes of everyone in the synagogue were fastened on Him, and He began by saying to them, "Today this scripture is fulfilled in your hearing." (Luke 4:16–21)

How God anointed Jesus of Nazareth with the Holy Spirit and power, and how He went around doing good and healing all who were under the power of the devil, because God was with Him. (Acts 10:38)

4. While many different people and things may be anointed, "Anointed One" frequently refers to the Messiah. In fact, the Hebrew word "Messiah" means "Anointed One." The Greek word "Christ" also means "Anointed One." So when we confess "Jesus Christ" we confess that He is the "Messiah" or the "Anointed One." Peter and John also make it clear in Acts 4:25–27 that Psalm 2 applies to Jesus. How does this make the first three verses of this psalm more significant?

You spoke by the Holy Spirit through the mouth of your servant, our father David:

'Why do the nations rage
and the peoples plot in vain?
The kings of the earth take their stand
and the rulers gather together
against the Lord
and against His Anointed One.'

Indeed Herod and Pontius Pilate met together with the Gentiles and the people of Israel in this city to conspire against your holy servant Jesus, whom you anointed. (Acts 4:25–27)

The Lord's Response—a King (verses 4–6)

1. Read verses 4–6. The kings and the rulers of the world may conspire against the Lord's anointed, but they fail to understand that there is a greater King than they. Who is that King and where is His kingdom? Read also Psalm 113:5; Isaiah 6:1; and Psalm 102:12.

Who is like the LORD our God,
the One who sits enthroned on high. (Psalm 113:5)

In the year that King Uzziah died, I saw the Lord seated on a throne, high and exalted, and the train of His robe filled the temple. (Isaiah 6:1)

But You, O LORD, sit enthroned forever;
Your renown endures through all generations. (Psalm 102:12)

2. Verses 4 and 5 show two different reactions of God to the schemes of a rebellious humanity. How does He respond? What does His response tell us about those opposed to Him? Read Job 38:4–5.

Where were you when I laid the earth's foundation?
Tell Me, if you understand.
Who marked off its dimensions? Surely you know!
Who stretched a measuring line across it? (Job 38:4–5)

3. When the nations rebel against God, He has one final response. What does God do on earth in response to the nations (verse 6)?

The King's Proclamation (verses 7–9)

1. Read verses 7–9. These verses take the form of a response by the king that God established on Zion's (another name for Jerusalem) throne. In these verses the king repeats words that God has spoken to him: "You are My Son, today I have become Your Father" (literally: "today I have begotten You"). This repeats the promise God made to David in 2 Samuel 7:11b–14a:

> The Lord declares to you that the Lord Himself will establish a house for you: When your days are over and you rest with your fathers, I will raise up your offspring to succeed you, who will come from your own body, and I will establish his kingdom. He is the one who will build a house for My Name, and I will establish the throne of his kingdom forever. I will be his Father, and he will be My son.

The New Testament repeatedly quotes verse 7 as applying to Christ. Read the following verses. What do they tell us about how Jesus fulfills this divine prophecy?

> And the Holy Spirit descended on Him in bodily form like a dove. And a voice came from heaven: "You are My Son, whom I love; with You I am well pleased." (Luke 3:22)

> While He was still speaking, a bright cloud enveloped them, and a voice from the cloud said, "This is My Son, whom I love; with Him I am well pleased. Listen to Him!" (Matthew 17:5)

> For to which of the angels did God ever say,
> "You are My Son; today I have become Your Father"? Or again,
> "I will be His Father, and He will be My Son"? (Hebrews 1:5)

> So Christ also did not take upon Himself the glory of becoming a high priest. But God said to Him, "You are My Son; today I have become Your Father." (Hebrews 5:5)

And who through the Spirit of holiness was declared with power to be the Son of God by His resurrection from the dead: Jesus Christ our Lord. (Romans 1:4)

2. The king (here referred to as the Anointed One) is also God's heir. What is his inheritance, according to verse 8? How is this powerfully and completely fulfilled in Christ? Read Matthew 28:18–20 and Acts 1:8.

Then Jesus came to them and said, "All authority in heaven and on earth has been given to Me. Therefore go and make disciples of all nations, baptizing them in the name of the Father and of the Son and of the Holy Spirit, and teaching them to obey everything I have commanded you. And surely I am with you always, to the very end of the age. (Matthew 28:18–20)

But you will receive power when the Holy Spirit comes on you; and you will be My witnesses in Jerusalem, and in all Judea and Samaria, and to the ends of the earth. (Acts 1:8)

3. In verse 9, it appears that the King will treat His inheritance differently than we might expect. How will He deal with this inheritance? Read Jeremiah 19:10–11 and Revelation 19:15.

Then break the jar while those who go with you are watching, and say to them, "This is what the LORD Almighty says: I will smash this nation and this city just as this potter's jar is smashed and cannot be repaired. They will bury the dead in Topheth until there is no more room." (Jeremiah 19:10–11)

Out of His mouth comes a sharp sword with which to strike down the nations. "He will rule them with an iron scepter." He treads the winepress of the fury of the wrath of God Almighty. (Revelation 19:15)

To the Nations: A Warning and Blessing (verses 10–12)

1. Read verses 10–12. If the psalm had ended with verse 9, it would be bleak and hopeless. But instead, God reaches out in love and mercy. These last verses show that the judgment prophesied will not necessarily fall on all people. Here the psalmist challenges his hearers to respond appropriately to what they have heard. Since the Lord has not yet carried out the judgement we deserve, what can we do?

2. The psalm ends with a promise. What is the promise? Does this affect our understanding of the psalm?

Applying the Message

1. In verse 3, the rebellious nations seek to throw off the chains and fetters of the Lord and His anointed. Do we ever view God's will as chains and fetters that restrict us from things we would like to do? Give examples of times we act this way.

2. The Lord laughs at, scoffs, and rebukes the plans of the rebellious of the world. Do we give Him cause to do these things to us? How do our actions demonstrate rebellion against God?

3. God's response to our rebellion is seen in the fulfillment of this psalm. The Lord establishes the King—His Son who is loved by God and will reign over all. See Philippians 2:9–11. He forgives us and gives us refuge. What might we do to thank Him for all of this?

4. Psalm 1 teaches us that we need to read the psalms from a faith perspective to fully understand this book. Psalm 2 likewise shows something essential to keep in mind when we read the psalms. What do you think this is?

Taking the Message Home

Review

Read Psalm 2 again. Remember that we have all rebelled against God and His Anointed One—the Christ. We have earned His laughter and scorn for our foolish reactions to His marvelous plans for our life. And yet, God doesn't destroy us—He sends us Christ to redeem us. God has covered us with Christ's righteousness and given us refuge in Him.

Looking Ahead

Next time we will look at the best known of all psalms—Psalm 23. Many people consider this one of their favorite parts of Scripture because of the rich picture of God's love and care for us. But, as Psalm 2 reminds us, we will understand it only through the person and work of Jesus.

Working Ahead

1. Read Psalm 23 and John 10:1–30. Reflect on the meaning of this psalm. When has it given you strength and encouragement? How does it depict the relationship our God establishes with us?

2. Psalm 23 has moved many people to depict its words in art, music, and poetry. How have you seen this psalm depicted through these and other media?

3. Read in a Bible dictionary or encyclopedia about shepherds. Describe the job of a shepherd.

Did You Know?

The Hebrew word *Selah* appears in 39 different psalms. It is also used in Habakkuk 3 (but that chapter is actually a psalm within the prophetic book). Despite all this use, scholars have not been able to determine the exact meaning of *Selah*. With just two exceptions, each psalm that contains the word also lists in its superscription the name of a melody or the type of psalm. Because of this, most scholars believe that *Selah* is a musical term of some kind. Some suggest that it calls for a musical interlude, a change in dynamics (probably an increase in volume), or a pause in the singing for narration; indicates that a response or refrain may be inserted; or provides instruction for some liturgical action. Because the word's exact meaning has not been determined, most Bible translations simply leave it in Hebrew—*Selah*.

Session 3

The Lord Our Shepherd

Psalm 23

Approaching This Study

Psalm 23 is without a doubt the best-known psalm and a favorite chapter of the Bible. It has comforted God's people for thousands of years. People often read it in times of crisis, when in need, or when grieving. In hospital beds and cemeteries it comforts troubled believers. We also read it in the happier times of life and remember that these times are gifts of our loving God.

When David wrote Psalm 23, he applied his faith to ordinary life experiences. David was a shepherd. As he tended his flock he realized that the care that he gave his sheep was, in a small way, reflective of the care that God gave to him. His relationship with God was so significant that it filled his entire life with meaning.

This psalm weaves all of these realities together in one consistent song: God is our Shepherd; He cares for us like a shepherd cares for his sheep; in good times and in bad, in plenty and in want He cares for us; He leads us, watches over us, and protects us. Certainly these are reasons for us to thank and praise Him!

An Overview

Everything in Psalm 23 expounds on one theme: the Lord our Shepherd. But as the psalm progresses, it reveals different elements of this metaphor. A basic pattern emerges:

The Shepherd Leads (verses 1–3)

The Shepherd Protects (verse 4)

The Shepherd Provides (verse 5)

The Faithful Shepherd (verse 6)

Working with the Text

The Shepherd Leads (verses 1–3)

1. Read Psalm 23:1–3. The chief image of this psalm compares God and His tender care to a shepherd who cares for his sheep. We are probably most familiar with the manner in which David renders this shepherd image, but many other passages of the Bible use the same image. How do Ezekiel 34:23; Isaiah 40:11; Ezekiel 34:11–13; and Psalm 23 help reveal God's work and His nature to us?

> I will place over them one Shepherd, My servant David, and He will tend them; He will tend them and be their Shepherd. (Ezekiel 34:23)

> He tends His flock like a shepherd:
> He gathers the lambs in His arms
> and carries them close to His heart;
> He gently leads those that have young. (Isaiah 40:11)

> For this is what the Sovereign LORD says: I Myself will search for My sheep and look after them. As a shepherd looks after his scattered flock when he is with them, so will I look after My sheep. I will rescue them from all the places where they were scattered on a day of clouds and darkness. I will bring them out from the nations and gather them from the countries, and I will bring them into their own land. I will pasture them on the mountains of Israel, in the ravines and in all the settlements in the land. (Ezekiel 34:11–13)

2. The prophecies of a Shepherd-Messiah are clearly fulfilled by Jesus Christ. Read the following passages. How do they clarify the full meaning of Psalm 23 for us?

> We all, like sheep, have gone astray,
> each of us has turned to his own way;
> and the LORD has laid on Him
> the iniquity of us all. (Isaiah 53:6)

When He saw the crowds, He had compassion on them, because they were harassed and helpless, like sheep without a shepherd. (Matthew 9:36)

I am the good shepherd. The good shepherd lays down His life for the sheep. … I am the good shepherd; I know My sheep and My sheep know Me. (John 10:11, 14)

3. David reminds us that because the Lord is our Shepherd, we "shall not be in want." Similar statements may be found in Psalm 34:9 and Philippians 4:19. David was in need many times in his life. There may be times when we may be in need. In light of this, what does this verse mean? How does this verse give us confidence even in difficult times?

Fear the LORD, you His saints,
for those who fear Him lack nothing. (Psalm 34:9)

And my God will meet all your needs according to His glorious riches in Christ Jesus. (Philippians 4:19)

4. As a shepherd cares for his sheep, God cares for us. What are the specific things that the Shepherd does for his sheep (verses 2 and 3)? How does God do these things for us not only physically but also spiritually?

5. Verse 3 says that the Shepherd "guides me in the paths of righteousness for His name's sake." It is not enough for a shepherd to feed his sheep; he has to move them safely from place to place. This verse might also be translated "He guides me in the right paths." Where does

our Shepherd guide us? How does He accomplish this? Why does He do these things?

The Shepherd Protects (verse 4)

1. Read verse 4. A shepherd who cares for his flock usually travels lightly. The two main tools that the shepherd uses are his rod and his staff. The rod is a short, strong club used as a weapon against predators. See 1 Samuel 17:34–35. The staff is a long, smooth shaft, often with a gentle hook at the end. The shepherd guides the sheep in the proper direction with his staff. The hook can be used to help a mother give birth to her lambs or to pull sheep back from extreme danger. David uses these two tools of the shepherd as a metaphor for the care of the Lord. How does God use a rod and a staff with us? How is this a comfort?

> But David said to Saul, "Your servant has been keeping his father's sheep. When a lion or a bear came and carried off a sheep from the flock, I went after it, struck it and rescued the sheep from its mouth. When it turned on me, I seized it by its hair, struck it and killed it." (1 Samuel 17:34–35)

2. The Shepherd's rod and staff are a comfort to David and to us. When walking through the "valley of the shadow of death," David "fears no evil." Why is he so confident? When have you felt as if you were in this valley? How can we cope with this situation?

The Shepherd Provides (verse 5)

1. Read verse 5. The images David uses change from those things

that a shepherd does for his sheep to those things that the Lord does for David and for us. What does it mean to prepare a table in the presence of one's enemies?

2. The second blessing of the Shepherd in this verse is that "He anoints my head with oil." In the time of the Old Testament, anointing was a common practice. People or objects were anointed to consecrate them for service to God or to show that God's power was upon them. The titles "Messiah" and "Christ" both mean "Anointed One." But people and animals were also anointed to soothe and heal their wounds. Read James 5:14 and Luke 10:34. What do you think it means to be anointed by the Shepherd? How does He anoint us as well?

> Is any one of you sick? He should call the elders of the church to pray over him and anoint him with oil in the name of the Lord. (James 5:14)

> He went to him and bandaged his wounds, pouring on oil and wine. Then he put the man on his own donkey, took him to an inn and took care of him. (Luke 10:34)

3. There is a third blessing indicated in verse 5. What does it mean when David says that his "cup overflows"? How does this reveal the amazing care of the Shepherd?

The Faithful Shepherd (verse 6)

1. Read verse 6. In this summary and conclusion to the psalm, how does David characterize the care of the Shepherd? How would a shep-

herd apply these attributes to his flock? How does God reveal these characteristics to us?

2. Because of all the things he mentions in this psalm and the many things he does not mention, David knows that he is safe and secure with the Lord as his Shepherd. How does he summarize the complete care of his Shepherd? How long will this care continue? Do we share in this same care? See also John 14:2.

> In My Father's house are many rooms; if it were not so, I would have told you. I am going there to prepare a place for you. (John 14:2)

Applying the Message

1. Look back over Psalm 23. David certainly speaks of the loving care of the Shepherd, but he presents it in different context. He especially prizes God's care because he finds it in difficult times—when he is in need, when he walks through the valley of the shadow of death (v. 4), and when his enemies surround him (v. 5). At these times, David learns to trust in the Lord and to see that all of his needs are more than provided for by his Shepherd. We also may be in need and face problems. What are some of the valleys through which we travel? Can we learn to deal with life's problems as David does in this psalm? What lessons might we learn from the psalm?

2. Perhaps Jesus was thinking of this psalm and of similar verses in the Old Testament when He referred to Himself as a Shepherd. Jesus

not only gives the kinds of care indicated in this psalm but even gives His own life to save His flock. Read John 10:11, 14 and Luke 15:4–7. How can these passages help us to see the full meaning of Psalm 23? Place yourself in the story of Luke 15. Can you see yourself as the lost sheep that the shepherd finds? Are there times when we are one of those who wait while the Shepherd finds other lost sheep? How can we better rejoice when our Shepherd brings another lost sheep home to safety?

> I am the good shepherd. The good shepherd lays down His life for the sheep. … I am the good shepherd; I know My sheep and My sheep know Me. (John 10:11, 14)

> Suppose one of you has a hundred sheep and loses one of them. Does he not leave the ninety-nine in the open country and go after the lost sheep until he finds it? And when he finds it, he joyfully puts it on his shoulders and goes home. Then he calls his friends and neighbors together and says, 'Rejoice with me; I have found my lost sheep.' I tell you that in the same way there will be more rejoicing in heaven over one sinner who repents than over ninety-nine righteous persons who do not need to repent. (Luke 15:4–7)

Taking the Message Home

Review

Read some other Bible passages that describe the Good Shepherd. Read Ezekiel 34 and its fulfillment in John 10:1–18, 25–30. Then read Revelation 7:13–17. Rejoice that you are one of God's sheep, and thank God for His abundant care for you and the whole church.

Looking Ahead

Next time we will study Psalm 139. This psalm describes God according to His attributes and then demonstrates how He uses those attributes on our behalf.

Working Ahead

1. Read Psalm 139. Notice how it describes God and His work on our behalf. How is this like the psalms we have already considered?

2. In Psalm 139 we will be talking about God's attributes. What are your attributes? How would you describe yourself? How would others describe you? Does knowing your characteristics help others to know you?

3. What are some of God's attributes? You may find it helpful to read the section on His attributes that is found in *Luther's Small Catechism with Explanation*, Concordia Publishing House, 1986, pp. 101–104.

Did You Know?

The Twenty-Third Psalm in Worship

Not only is Psalm 23 one of the most popular psalms and chapters of Scripture—many composers have based musical compositions on it. In addition to hymns which are closely related to it, *Lutheran Worship* presents four different musical settings of this psalm: (1) the chant tone (pp. 320–321), (2) "The King of Love My Shepherd Is" (*LW* 412), (3) "The Lord's My Shepherd, I'll Not Want" (*LW* 416), and (4) "The Lord's My Shepherd, Leading Me" (*LW* 417). Look at the way each of these songs render the first stanza of the psalm. Better yet, open your hymnal and sing along!

Chant (New International Version)	The King of Love My Shepherd Is, *LW* 412
The LORD is my shepherd, I shall lack nothing. He makes me lie down in green pastures, He leads me beside quiet waters.	The King of love my shepherd is, Whose goodness faileth never; I nothing lack if I am His And He is mine forever Where streams of living water flow, My ransomed soul He leadeth And, where the verdant pastures grow, With food celestial feedeth.

The Lord's My Shepherd, I'll Not Want, *LW* 416	The Lord's My Shepherd, Leading Me, *LW* 417
The Lord's my shepherd, I'll not want; He makes me down to lie In pastures green; He leadeth me The quiet waters by.	The Lord's my shepherd, leading me To pastures newly green; Deep flow the waters of His care, His mercies unforeseen. He loves me so, He leads me to His pastures gently green.

(From *Lutheran Worship.* Copyright © 1982 Concordia Publishing House. All rights reserved. Words of stanza 1 of the song "The Lord's My Shepherd, Leading Me" © 1981 Henry L. Letterman, 1932–1996.)

Session 4

God's Attributes

Psalm 139

Approaching This Study

How do you introduce yourself to someone you don't know? What words do you use to describe yourself? Perhaps you mention your family, your occupation, or places you have lived. We often tell other people things that we do or have done.

As you share who you are, the other person begins to know you. The other person is apt to learn not only your history and your likes and dislikes but also what *you* are like.

We can learn a great deal about our Lord in His Word—the Bible. We learn His names. These names tell us a lot about God. We learn about things that He has done and continues to do. And we learn His attributes—things that describe His nature. When we know these attributes, we know Him better. And when we know these attributes, we learn how He uses them in our life. We will learn about some of these attributes in Psalm 139.

An Overview

Psalm 139 focuses directly on two of God's attributes: His omniscience (perfect knowledge) and His omnipresence (He is always present everywhere). These attributes are then applied to His relationship to people. The psalm might be outlined:

The Knowledge of God (verses 1–6)

The Presence of God (verses 7–12)

God's Involvement in Individual Lives (verses 13–18)

A Plea for God's Action on Our Behalf (verses 19–24)

Working with the Text

The Knowledge of God (verses 1–6)

1. Read Psalm 139:1–6. These verses proclaim that God possesses great knowledge of the psalmist. How does God know these things? What does this level of knowledge tell us about God?

2. The psalmist uses poetic language to demonstrate that there are no limits to God's knowledge. He conveys God's complete knowledge of his life by relating seven of the things that God knows about him. What are they, and how do they reveal God's knowledge?

3. Reread verse 5. God "hems me in" or encloses me behind and before. Does the psalmist think this behavior is positive or negative? Why? See also Psalm 125:2 and Psalm 34:7.

As the mountains surround Jerusalem,
so the Lord surrounds His people
both now and forevermore. (Psalm 125:2)

The angel of the Lord encamps around those who fear Him, and He delivers them. (Psalm 34:7)

4. Verses 1–5 are summarized in verse 6. How does God's knowledge compare to our knowledge? Is this positive or negative? Why? See also Romans 11:33 and Job 42:3b.

Oh, the depth of the riches of the wisdom and knowledge of God!
How unsearchable His judgments,
and His paths beyond tracing out! (Romans 11:33)

Surely I spoke of things I did not understand,
things too wonderful for me to know. (Job 42:3b)

The Presence of God (verses 7–12)

1. Read verses 7–12. Having described God's omniscience, the psalmist now proceeds to reveal His omnipresence. How does the psalmist demonstrate the presence of God? Where can God be found? Where can we go to hide from God? See also Jeremiah 23:24.

"Can anyone hide in secret places
so that I cannot see him?"
declares the LORD.
"Do not I fill heaven and earth?"
declares the LORD. (Jeremiah 23:24)

2. As with verse 5, some consider God's omnipresence negative. When might we want to escape from the presence of God?

3. It is unlikely the psalmist wishes to frighten us with the knowledge of God's presence. Instead, the psalmist sees God's omnipresence as a great comfort. How might God's continual presence comfort us today?

God's Involvement in Individual Lives (verses 13–18)

1. Read verses 13–18. The psalmist now draws our attention away from God's attributes as demonstrated throughout the universe to His actions in a single life—our own. How do these verses demonstrate God's concern for each person? See also Isaiah 44:24.

> This is what the LORD says—
> your Redeemer, who formed you in the womb:
> I am the LORD,
> who has made all things,
> who alone stretched out the heavens,
> who spread out the earth by Myself. (Isaiah 44:24)

2. The psalmist describes himself as being "fearfully and wonderfully made." What do these words mean? What action by God would cause the psalmist to describe his existence as fearful and wonderful? How has modern scientific knowledge made this even more obvious?

3. Verse 16 tells us that God's knowledge applies to our life. At what point in our life does God begin planning for us? What does this tell us about the dignity and value that God gives to each human being? What does it tell you about your value?

4. As verse 6 tells us we cannot attain God's depth of knowledge, so verses 17 and 18 remind us of the same thing. Why did the psalmist repeat this idea? How does the truth of these verses lead you to confess that our knowledge cannot compare to the depth of God's knowledge?

A Plea for God's Action on Our Behalf (verses 19–24)

1. Read verses 19–24. These verses challenge us. The word "hate" in Hebrew may also mean "reject." Still, the psalmist says that he wants God to "slay the wicked" (verse 19). What reason does he give for this request? See also 2 Chronicles 19:2.

> Jehu, the seer, the son of Hanani, went out to meet him and said to the king, "Should you help the wicked and love those who hate the LORD? Because of this, the wrath of the LORD is upon you." (2 Chronicles 19:2)

2. While the psalmist does call for God's judgment on the wicked, he also calls for God to examine him again. What does the psalmist do to keep from being counted among the wicked?

Applying the Message

1. This psalm speaks very clearly about God's gracious actions in our life both before and after our birth. How might these verses help us to explain God's teaching concerning the life of the unborn to our society? How might we help to support the lives of the unborn?

2. The psalmist speaks very harshly regarding God's enemies. Even as they deserve His judgment, we also have been the enemies of God and deserve His judgment. How does our Lord deal with His enemies? How has He dealt with us? How would He have us deal with our enemies?

3. Psalm 139 describes God's omniscience and omnipresence and how they relate to our life. How may these attributes of God comfort us today?

Taking the Message Home

Review

Read Psalm 139 again. God is omniscient and omnipresent and uses these attributes for our benefit. Consider also some of God's other attributes and how He uses them on our behalf. Some of God's other attributes are that He is omnipotent (all-powerful), holy, immutable (unchanging), eternal, wise, good, loving, truthful, and patient. What a marvelous God we have!

Looking Ahead

Next time we will look at Psalm 51—a psalm of confession. Against God's holiness we see our sin and our need for His mercy and forgiveness. God's response: His gracious love.

Working Ahead

1. Read Psalm 51.

2. Read the story of David and Bathsheba in 2 Samuel 11:1–12:24. What were David's offenses? If someone did the things to your family that David did, how would you respond?

3. Read the order for Confession and Absolution in your hymnal. Notice the kinds of things we confess before God. Experience His amazing response to our confession.

Did You Know?

Authorship of the Psalms

The most prolific psalm writer was David. Seventy-three different psalms are ascribed to him. The second most productive writer doesn't approach the extent of David's authorship. Asaph wrote 12 of the psalms. Eleven are ascribed to the Sons of Korah (though the psalms may have been written either for or by them). Solomon's name appears on two. Heman and Ethan each authored one of the psalms. One of them comes to us from Moses. The remaining 50 psalms are of unknown authorship.

Session 5

Have Mercy on Me: A Sinner!

Psalm 51

Approaching This Study

King David is a well-known Old Testament figure. When he was just a boy he fought against the Philistine giant, Goliath, and killed this warrior with a stone thrown from a sling. He served in the court of King Saul and later succeeded Saul on the throne. As king, David did remarkable things. He captured Jerusalem and made it the capital city. He expanded the territory of Israel. He prepared a site and acquired the materials needed to build God's temple, a structure completed by his son, Solomon.

1 Kings 15:5 says, "David had done what was right in the eyes of the LORD and had not failed to keep any of the LORD's commands all the days of his life—except in the case of Uriah the Hittite." That is the problem addressed in Psalm 51. 2 Samuel 11–12 tells how David looked down from his palace and saw a woman named Bathsheba bathing. He desired this beautiful woman, so he called her to the palace where he committed adultery with her. Her husband, Uriah the Hittite, fought in David's army. When Bathsheba became pregnant, David called Uriah back to Jerusalem, hoping that he would sleep with his wife and think that her baby was his. When this didn't happen, David gave orders that ensured Uriah's death in battle.

After the customary time of mourning had passed, David married Bathsheba and she gave birth to his son. The Lord was displeased with David's actions. He sent the prophet Nathan to confront David. David learned that trouble would fill his house and that his son would die. Confronted with the horrible reality of his sin, David repented and confessed his sin to the Lord. Psalm 51 is his confession.

An Overview

Psalm 51 contains the words of someone who knows that he has no right to ask for forgiveness. He deserves punishment, and yet he pleads for God's undeserved mercy and love. In this psalm we see what God desires of us and His response to repentant sinners. This psalm contains three main sections framed by a two-verse introduction and conclusion.

Introduction: Have Mercy! (verses 1–2)

Confession (verses 3–6)

Prayer for Forgiveness and Renewal (verses 7–12)

Promise to Praise (verses 13–17)

Conclusion: Prayer for Zion (verses 18–19)

Working with the Text

Introduction: Have Mercy! (verses 1–2)

1. Read Psalm 51:1–2. The heading of this psalm tells us that David wrote it and the occasion for its writing. Summarize what you discovered from reading 2 Samuel 11:1–12:24. David writes this psalm of repentance in response to those events. What specific sins caused David to write this psalm? What punishment do you think David deserved for his actions? For what does he plead instead? See also Luke 18:13. On what does David base his request?

> But the tax collector stood at a distance. He would not even look up to heaven, but beat his breast and said, "God, have mercy on me, a sinner." (Luke 18:13)

2. After pleading for mercy, David repeats his request for forgiveness three times. For what does he seek forgiveness? What does he ask God to do? What do each of these images communicate?

Confession (verses 3–6)

1. Read verses 3–6. David is fully aware of the extent of his sin because his sin is "always before him." He may have meant this quite literally. His adultery had produced a child, and that child was a constant reminder of his sinful act. Moreover, the guilt of his sin is strongly on his mind. Who does David say he sinned against in verse 4? Who does he appear to sin against in 2 Samuel 11:4, 16–17? What do these verses tell us about sin? Against whom do we really sin? See also Luke 15:18.

> Then David sent messengers to get [Bathsheba]. She came to him, and he slept with her. (She had purified herself from her uncleanness.) Then she went back home. … While Joab had the city under siege, he put Uriah at a place where he knew the strongest defenders were. When the men of the city came out and fought against Joab, some of the men in David's army fell; moreover, Uriah the Hittite died. (2 Samuel 11:4, 16–17)

> I will set out and go back to my father and say to him: Father, I have sinned against heaven and against you. (Luke 15:18)

2. If all our sin is ultimately against God, what do we deserve (verse 4)?

3. David's confession is sincere and complete. He does not make excuses but pleads for mercy. What startling statement does he make in verse 5? What is the significance of this statement for David? For our sinfulness? Can anyone escape this condemnation?

4. Even in his sin-filled condition, David recognizes God's desire for him. What does verse 6 tell us that God wants of us?

Prayer for Forgiveness and Renewal (verses 7–12)

1. Read verses 7–12. Here David uses the same metaphors for forgiveness that he uses in verses 1 and 2, but he reverses the order and lets us see the outcome. David asks God to cleanse him with hyssop—a type of brush found in Palestine that was used in some Old Testament religious rites. How was hyssop used in Leviticus 14:4–7; Exodus 12:22–23; and John 19:28–30? How do these verses help explain the meaning of Psalm 51:7?

> The priest shall order that two live clean birds and some cedar wood, scarlet yarn and hyssop be brought for the one to be cleansed. Then the priest shall order that one of the birds be killed over fresh water in a clay pot. He is then to take the live bird and dip it, together with the cedar wood, the scarlet yarn and the hyssop, into the blood of the bird that was killed over the fresh water. Seven times he shall sprinkle the one to be cleansed of the infectious disease and pronounce him clean. Then he is to release the live bird in the open fields. (Leviticus 14:4–7)

> Take a bunch of hyssop, dip it into the blood in the basin and put some of the blood on the top and on both sides of the doorframe. Not one of you shall go out the door of his house until morning. When the LORD goes through the land to strike down the Egyptians, He will see the blood on the top and sides of the doorframe and will pass over that doorway, and He will not permit the destroyer to enter your houses and strike you down. (Exodus 12:22–23)

> Later, knowing that all was now completed, and so that the Scripture would be fulfilled, Jesus said, "I am thirsty." A jar of wine vinegar was there, so they soaked a sponge in it, put the sponge on a stalk of the hyssop plant, and lifted it to Jesus' lips. When He had received the drink, Jesus said, "It is finished." With that, He bowed His head and gave up His spirit. (John 19:28–30)

2. In verses 7–9, David repeats his request from verses 1–2 but in reverse order. What does he now ask of the Lord in verse 10? What is the only way God can fulfill his request? See also Matthew 15:19–20a; Jeremiah 24:7; and Ezekiel 36:26.

For out of the heart come evil thoughts, murder, adultery, sexual immorality, theft, false testimony, slander. These are what make a man unclean. (Matthew 15:19–20a)

I will give them a heart to know Me, that I am the LORD. They will be My people, and I will be their God, for they will return to Me with all their heart. (Jeremiah 24:7)

I will give you a new heart and put a new spirit in you; I will remove from you your heart of stone and give you a heart of flesh. (Ezekiel 36:26)

3. David has pleaded to God to do things for him. In verse 11 he pleads that God refrain from doing two things. What are they? Would it be fair for God to do them? Does God want to do these things? See also Romans 8:9 and 1 Corinthians 12:3.

You, however, are controlled not by the sinful nature but by the Spirit, if the Spirit of God lives in you. And if anyone does not have the Spirit of Christ, he does not belong to Christ. (Romans 8:9)

Therefore I tell you that no one who is speaking by the Spirit of God says, "Jesus be cursed," and no one can say, "Jesus is Lord," except by the Holy Spirit. (1 Corinthians 12:3)

4. David has asked unimaginable things from God. He has two more requests in verse 12. What does he seek? How do these requests follow from what he has already asked?

Promise to Praise (verses 13–17)

1. Read verses 13–17. In these verses David makes promises to God. Notice that his promises don't come until late in the psalm. He has already confessed his sin and asked for God's forgiveness and blessing. David does not make a deal with God but responds to His grace and mercy. What are the three promises that David makes in response to God's grace? How do these demonstrate that God has changed David's heart?

2. How do verses 16 and 17 demonstrate the proper response to sin? Does God want us to "pay Him back" for the damage we have done?

Conclusion: Prayer for Zion (verse 18–19)

1. Read verses 18–19. At first glance these verses do not seem to fit with this psalm. But if we remember that the psalm was written by a repentant king, it makes more sense. Why does the king ask God to make Zion prosper and to build up the walls of Jerusalem?

2. Verse 16 said that God does not delight in sacrifices or take pleasure in burnt offerings, and yet verse 19 says there will be righteous sacrifices and whole burnt offerings to delight God. Do these verses contradict each other? How do they complement each other to give us a full understanding?

Applying the Message

1. David was tempted to believe that there was a limit to God's forgiveness. Christians may be tempted to believe the same thing. What are the limits to God's forgiveness? Are our sins ever so great that God cannot forgive them? Does this psalm support your answer? What would you tell someone who had a hard time believing that God could forgive them?

2. Since Psalm 51 speaks so powerfully to our human condition and the grace of God, believers have used it in worship for centuries. You may recognize several parts of this psalm from the church's liturgy. What verses appear in the worship of the church? How are they used? What does this use tell us?

3. In verse 12, David pleads, *"Restore to me the joy of Your salvation."* Perhaps we, like David, have lost the joy of our salvation. How might God once again restore the joy?

Taking the Message Home

Review

Read Psalm 51 again, putting yourself into the words. We do not come before God to repent of David's sin but our own. What sins have you committed that trouble you? What have you done to disrupt your relationship with God? From what do you need to be cleansed? Don't forget that sin is not only what we do but also what we are. Then read the psalm and speak the words as your own. Wash me, cleanse me, blot out all my iniquities. Know the forgiveness that God promises you through Jesus Christ. Then let God fill you with the joy of our salvation!

Looking Ahead

Next time we will study Psalm 95. You may recognize part of this psalm of praise from our worship. Having confessed our sins with Psalm 51 and having heard God's forgiveness, Psalm 95 is certainly an appropriate response to God for His goodness.

Working Ahead

1. Read Psalm 95.

2. Psalm 95 deals with the events that occurred in Exodus 17:1–7. Read these verses and summarize what happens in them.

3. Psalm 95 will refer to two places: Meribah and Massah. If possible, look them up in a Bible Dictionary and see what you can discover about them.

Did You Know?

Acrostic Psalms

One of the more interesting types of psalms is the acrostic psalm. In this type of writing, the author writes based on a predetermined sequence of beginning letters. One of the more familiar examples to us is a poem that describes a mother. The first line begins "M is for the many things she gave me." The second line begins with an O. In six lines the word "mother" is spelled out by the initial letter of the line. Several psalms are based on acrostics. Here they follow the order of the Hebrew alphabet. These include Psalms 25, 34, 37, 111, 112, and 145. The most significant example of this is the longest psalm, Psalm 119. This psalm follows an acrostic pattern, using each letter of the Hebrew alphabet to begin eight consecutive verses until the entire alphabet has been used. The names of the Hebrew letters are used as paragraph headings in many modern translations.

Session 6

An Invitation to Worship

Psalm 95

Approaching the Study

Psalm 95 celebrates God's universal reign over all things and applies this to our life. Knowing God, His gracious work towards us, and His glory and might, we are called to worship Him. We can easily imagine this psalm used in the corporate worship of the temple. To this day, Christians use it in worship.

This psalm has no introductory information. We are not told the type of song, the instruments, or the melody. Neither does the psalm tell us its author. The Book of Hebrews quotes this psalm, introducing it with the words "as the Holy Spirit says" (Hebrews 3:7), which reminds us again that all Scripture is inspired by God. It is God's Word. Hebrews also says that in this psalm "He spoke through David" (4:7). While this seems to indicate clearly that David authored the psalm, the writer of Hebrews may have followed the Jewish custom of ascribing all of the psalter to David.

This psalm calls us to worship. As we study, don't forget to make this a time of worship as well, rejoicing in the wonder of our God!

An Overview

Psalm 95 has two major sections: a call to worship in the first seven verses, and a warning against unbelief in the last verses. The division is actually in the middle of verse 7 (which splits a sentence). To aid our understanding, we'll divide the psalm into four different subparts:

An Invitation to Worship (verses 1–2)

God's Supremacy over All Things (verses 3–5)

God's Action in Our Life (verses 6–7a)

Warning against Unbelief (verses 7b–11)

Working with the Text

An Invitation to Worship (verses 1–2)

1. Read Psalm 95:1–2. These verses use parallelism to invite us to worship God. What four descriptions of worship does the author use in these verses? What does each mean?

2. Verse 1 describes the Lord as "the Rock of our salvation." What does this description tell us about God? See also Psalm 18:2; 2 Samuel 22:47; Exodus 33:21–22; Exodus 17:6; and 1 Corinthians 10:4. How do these verses help us understand what it means for God to be our Rock?

> The LORD is my rock, my fortress and my deliverer;
> my God is my rock, in whom I take refuge.
> He is my shield and the horn of my salvation, my stronghold.
> (Psalm 18:2)

> The LORD lives! Praise be to my Rock!
> Exalted be God, the Rock, my Savior! (2 Samuel 22:47)

> Then the LORD said, "There is a place near Me where you may stand on a rock. When My glory passes by, I will put you in a cleft in the rock and cover you with My hand until I have passed by." (Exodus 33:21–22)

> [The Lord said,] "I will stand there before you by the rock at Horeb. Strike the rock, and water will come out of it for the people to drink." So Moses did this in the sight of the elders of Israel. (Exodus 17:6)

> [Our fathers] drank from the spiritual rock that accompanied them, and that rock was Christ. (1 Corinthians 10:4)

God's Supremacy over All Things (verses 3–5)

1. Read verses 3–5. While the first two verses of this psalm call us to worship, these verses give us two specific reasons why we should worship. What is the reason for worship given in verse 3?

2. What does it mean to call God "the great King above all gods?" See also Psalm 96:4–5; Jeremiah 10:11, 14–15; and Isaiah 44:8.

> For great is the LORD and most worthy of praise;
> He is to be feared above all gods.
> For all the gods of the nations are idols,
> but the LORD made the heavens. (Psalm 96:4–5)

> Tell them this: "These gods, who did not make the heavens
> and the earth, will perish from the earth and from under the
> heavens." …
> Everyone is senseless and without knowledge;
> every goldsmith is shamed by his idols.
> His images are a fraud;
> they have no breath in them.
> They are worthless, the objects of mockery;
> when their judgment comes, they will perish. (Jeremiah 10:11,
> 14–15)

> Do not tremble, do not be afraid.
> Did I not proclaim this and foretell it long ago?
> You are My witnesses. Is there any God besides Me?
> No, there is no other Rock; I know not one. (Isaiah 44:8)

3. Verses 4 and 5 provide another reason to worship. What is this reason? What other evidence can you provide to support this reason?

God's Action in Our Life (verses 6–7a)

1. Read verses 6–7a (stop before "Today …"). The first two verses of this psalm call us to an exuberant, loud, and joyful worship. How would you characterize the worship called for in verse 6? How does this worship and that mentioned at the beginning of the psalm fit together? What reason does verse 6 give for us to worship? See also Isaiah 43:1.

But now, this is what the LORD says—
He who created you, O Jacob,
He who formed you, O Israel:
Fear not, for I have redeemed you;
I have summoned you by name; you are Mine. (Isaiah 43:1)

2. Verse 7 provides us one more reason to worship God. What is this reason? What does this image of our God teach us about Him and of our relationship to Him? See also Psalm 79:13; Psalm 100:3; and Psalm 23:1.

Then we Your people, the sheep of Your pasture,
will praise You forever;
from generation to generation
we will recount Your praise. (Psalm 79:13)

Know that the LORD is God.
It is He who made us, and we are His;
we are His people, the sheep of His pasture. (Psalm 100:3)

The LORD is my shepherd, I shall lack nothing. (Psalm 23:1)

Warning against Unbelief (Verses 7b–11)

1. Read verse 7b–11. The tone of the psalm changes from a call to worship to a warning: "Do not harden your hearts." What does this mean? See also Exodus 8:15 and Daniel 5:20.

But when Pharaoh saw that there was relief, he hardened his heart and would not listen to Moses and Aaron, just as the LORD had said. (Exodus 8:15)

But when his heart became arrogant and hardened with pride, he was deposed from his royal throne and stripped of his glory. (Daniel 5:20)

2. The psalmist uses an incident that took place at Meribah and Massah as an example of hardened hearts. Meribah means "strife" and Massah means "testing." What happened in this place that caused it to be given these names? See Exodus 17:1–7. How is this a good example of hardened hearts?

The whole Israelite community set out from the Desert of Sin, traveling from place to place as the LORD commanded. They camped at Rephidim, but there was no water for the people to drink. So they quarreled with Moses and said, "Give us water to drink." Moses replied, "Why do you quarrel with me? Why do you put the LORD to the test?" But the people were thirsty for water there, and they grumbled against Moses. They said, "Why did you bring us up out of Egypt to make us and our children and livestock die of thirst?" Then Moses cried out to the LORD, "What am I to do with these people? They are almost ready to stone me." The LORD answered Moses, "Walk on ahead of the people. Take with you some of the elders of Israel and take in your hand the staff with which you struck the Nile, and go. I will stand there before you by the rock at Horeb. Strike the rock, and water will come out of it for the people to drink." So Moses did this in the sight of the elders of Israel. And he called the place Massah and Meribah because the Israelites quarreled and because they tested the LORD saying, "Is the LORD among us or not?" (Exodus 17:1–7)

3. The Book of Hebrews (chapters 3–4) quotes this section of Psalm 95 in order to remind us of its warning. See Hebrews 3:12–13. Are we in danger of hardening our hearts? What can be done to keep us from doing this?

See to it, brothers, that none of you has a sinful, unbelieving heart that turns away from the living God. But encourage one another daily, as long as it is called Today, so that none of you may be hardened by sin's deceitfulness. (Hebrews 3:12–13)

4. As a consequence of Israel's repeated rebellion against God, Psalm 95 reminds us that the people wandered in the desert for 40 years before they reached the Promised Land. When Israel finally entered the Promised Land, who did not enter? What did they lose because of their grumbling? Who did receive these things? See also Numbers 14:23, 28–30.

Not one of them will ever see the land I promised on oath to their forefathers. No one who has treated Me with contempt will ever see it. So tell them, "As surely as I live, declares the LORD, I will do to you the very things I heard you say: In this desert your bodies will fall—every one of you twenty years old or more who was counted in the census and who has grumbled against Me. Not one of you will enter the land I swore with uplifted hand to make your home, except Caleb son of Jephunneh and Joshua son of Nun." (Numbers 14:23, 28–30)

Applying the Message

1. Many people are familiar with Psalm 95 because of its use in the Christian liturgy. For centuries, the Christian church has sung the service of Matins or Morning Prayer. This service calls for the singing (or

speaking) of the psalms on a rotating basis. But the first portion of Psalm 95 (verses 1–7a) is always included in Matins. This selection is called the *Venite* (Latin for "O come," the first words of this psalm). What makes this psalm a particularly good choice for regular use in worship? How might we use this psalm as a pattern for our regular worship?

2. This psalm undergoes a change in tone and focus in verse 7. The psalmist introduces the section of warning with the words "today, if you hear His voice, do not harden your hearts." Why does he begin this warning with the word "today"? See also Hebrews 3:13 and 2 Corinthians 6:2b. What can we learn from this?

> But encourage one another daily, as long as it is called Today, so that none of you may be hardened by sin's deceitfulness. (Hebrews 3:13)

> I tell you, now is the time of God's favor, now is the day of salvation. (2 Corinthians 6:2b)

3. As a warning to us, this psalm reminds us that those who rebelled against God did not enter the promised rest but spent their life wandering in the desert. If we do not harden our hearts against Him, what does God promise? See Hebrews 4:3a; Matthew 11:28–29; and Revelation 14:13. How is this a comforting promise?

> Now we who have believed enter that rest, just as God has said. (Hebrews 4:3a)

> Come to Me, all you who are weary and burdened, and I will give you rest. Take My yoke upon you and learn from Me, for I am gentle and humble in heart, and you will find rest for your souls. (Matthew 11:28–29)

> Then I heard a voice from heaven say, "Write: Blessed are the dead who die in the Lord from now on." "Yes," says the Spirit,

"they will rest from their labor, for their deeds will follow them."
(Revelation 14:13)

Taking the Message Home

Review

Psalm 95 is a wonderful psalm of praise, but it doesn't stand alone. Compare Psalm 95 to Psalm 81. Look at all the parallels between these psalms. How are they similar? How are they different?

Psalms 95–100 are all psalms of praise. Read several of these psalms this week. Let them lead you to praise God for all that He has done, especially the rest He has promised to provide through our faith in Jesus when we pass from this life into eternal life in heaven.

Looking Ahead

Next time we will look at a messianic psalm. Psalm 22 prophesies vividly of the work of Jesus Christ as He suffered on the cross for us.

Working Ahead

1. Read Psalm 22.

2. What does it mean to be forsaken? Have you ever felt truly alone? How do you react to this feeling?

3. Jesus was forsaken on the cross. Read Matthew 27:32–54 and reflect on the depth of His suffering. He suffered for us physically and mentally so that we might not be alone and forsaken!

Did You Know?

Instruments to Accompany the Psalms

The psalms were written to be sung, and they were often sung to musical accompaniment of some type. Some of the psalms give instructions for what kinds of instruments should be used. While the precise meaning of some Hebrew words is unclear, the most common instrumentation includes stringed instruments, flutes, and lyres. When we read the psalms we also find, within their verses, references to a number of other instruments to be used in God's praise. Among the most notable examples of this are the following two examples:

> make music to the LORD with the harp,
> with the harp and the sound of singing,
> with trumpets and the blast of the ram's horn—
> shout for joy before the LORD, the King. (Psalm 98:5–6)

> Praise Him with the sounding of the trumpet,
> praise Him with the harp and lyre,
> praise Him with tambourine and dancing,
> praise Him with the strings and flute,
> praise Him with the clash of cymbals,
> praise Him with resounding cymbals.
> Let everything that has breath praise the LORD.
> Praise the LORD. (Psalm 150:3–6)

Session 7

The Suffering Messiah

Psalm 22

Approaching This Study

God had chosen David to be the second king of Israel. The first king, Saul, who we read about in 1 Samuel 9–31, was at first popular with the people who had demanded a king. But this king was not faithful to God. Three times Saul disqualified himself from office, so God rejected him as king and chose another—David.

God first identified David as the king-elect in very unusual circumstances. He was the youngest of Jesse's sons and had been out tending sheep. The prophet Nathan came to him and anointed him with oil (1 Samuel 16). But David was young, and Saul continued to serve as king. Saul chose David to serve as a sort of court musician (1 Samuel 16:17–21). While serving the temperamental Saul, David went out to the battlefields one day and heard the challenge of the Philistine giant-warrior, Goliath. David killed Goliath with God's power, and the Israelites were victorious. Returning home, the Israelites greeted the soldiers with the cry, *"Saul has slain his thousands, and David his tens of thousands"* (1 Samuel 18:7). Saul grew increasingly jealous of David.

Stories of how Saul turned on David fill 1 Samuel. Saul cheated David, reduced him in military rank, and tried to kill him. David ran for his life. Eventually, Saul died and David succeeded him as king. David wrote Psalm 22 at a time when Saul pursued him. God had chosen him as king, and as a result his life was threatened. David cried to the Lord for help. At the same time, David wrote prophetically. His greatest descendant, Jesus Christ, would speak the same words as He was persecuted—on the cross.

An Overview

In Psalm 22 David wrestles with the difficult topic of human suffering. We see David suffering—the suffering that he overcomes with God's aid. We see Jesus suffering—the greatest suffering and death that He conquers in His resurrection. We, too, face suffering, but God strengthens us to overcome. In simultaneously revealing the suffering faced by David and by Jesus, Psalm 22 can be divided into four parts:

Forsaken by God? (verses 1–5)

The World Mocks (verses 6–11)

The Depth of Suffering (verses 12–21)

God's Deliverance (verses 22–31)

Working with the Text

Forsaken by God? (verses 1–5)

1. Read verses 1–5. Describe the mood of the speaker in verses 1 and 2. What are his chief complaints?

2. While hanging on the cross, Jesus quotes verse 1 in Aramaic. "About the ninth hour Jesus cried out in a loud voice, 'Eloi, Eloi, lama sabachthani?'—which means, 'My God, My God, why have You forsaken Me?' " (Matthew 27:46) How does this change our understanding of this psalm? What does it mean for Jesus to be forsaken by God?

3. Though he feels forsaken, the writer does not forget about God's help in the past. What evidence does he give of God's power?

The World Mocks (verses 6–11)

1. Read verses 6–11. The psalmist knows that God is holy and powerful. How does he describe himself in verse 6? What does this mean?

2. Other biblical writers use similar descriptions. How do Isaiah 41:14 and Job 25:6 help us understand the meaning of this verse?

"Do not be afraid, O worm Jacob, O little Israel, for I Myself will help you," declares the LORD, your Redeemer, the Holy One of Israel. (Isaiah 41:14)

How much less man, who is but a maggot— a son of man, who is only a worm! (Job 25:6)

3. David describes himself as "a worm and not a man." How do people treat him so that he thinks this way? How is this seen in the crucifixion of Jesus? See Matthew 27:39–44.

Those who passed by hurled insults at Him, shaking their heads and saying, "You who are going to destroy the temple and build it in three days, save Yourself! Come down from the cross, if You are the Son of God!" In the same way the chief priests, the teachers of the law and the elders mocked Him. "He saved others," they said, "but He can't save Himself! He's the King of Israel! Let Him come down now from the cross, and we will believe in Him. He trusts in God. Let God rescue Him now if He wants Him, for He said, 'I am the Son of God.' " In the same way the robbers who were crucified with Him also heaped insults on Him. (Matthew 27:39–44)

4. When facing the mocking of the world, what reassures the writer (vv. 9–10)?

5. At what point in his life did the psalmist's relationship with God begin? Who instigated this relationship?

The Depth of Suffering (verses 12–21)

1. Read verses 12–21. Bashan is a region east of the Jordan River that was known for its good pastures and, therefore, good cattle. David describes his enemies as attacking animals. Verse 12 describes his enemies as strong bulls surrounding him—verse 13, as lions that seek to eat him. Verse 16 describes them as dogs, scavengers who eat what other animals leave behind. Ultimately, verse 16 makes it clear that the enemies who surround him are human—the worst type of enemy. Faced with these adversaries, what has happened to the writer physically and emotionally?

2. How do these verses prefigure the crucifixion of Christ?

a. Verse 14b—"All my bones are out of joint"; Verse 17a—"I can count all my bones."

b. Verse 15—"My strength is dried up like a potsherd, and my tongue sticks to the roof of my mouth." See also John 19:28.

Later, knowing that all was now completed, and so that the Scripture would be fulfilled, Jesus said, "I am thirsty." (John 19:28)

c. Verse 16c—"They have pierced my hands and my feet." See also John 20:25.

> So the other disciples told him, "We have seen the Lord!" But he said to them, "Unless I see the nail marks in His hands and put my finger where the nails were, and put my hand into His side, I will not believe it." (John 20:25)

d. Verse 18—"They divide my garments among them and cast lots for my clothing." See also John 19:23–24.

> When the soldiers crucified Jesus, they took His clothes, dividing them into four shares, one for each of them, with the undergarment remaining. This garment was seamless, woven in one piece from top to bottom. "Let's not tear it," they said to one another. "Let's decide by lot who will get it." This happened that the scripture might be fulfilled which said, "They divided My garments among them and cast lots for My clothing." So this is what the soldiers did. (John 19:23–24)

3. Even while facing all of these sufferings and indignities, the speaker has not given up hope. What does he ask in verse 19–21?

God's Deliverance (verses 22–31)

1. Read verses 22–26. It seems from this last section that the prayers of David have been answered, and that he has been delivered. He turns from a cry for help to a cry of praise, and summons all who believe in the Lord to praise Him. What are the reasons for this praise?

2. This psalm powerfully prophesies of the crucifixion of Jesus. Jesus even quotes the first verse while He is crucified. Do these verses apply to Jesus also? Was Jesus delivered, or did His prayer go unanswered?

3. Read verses 27–31. After David calls his people to praise and honor God for all that He has done, he notes that the praise will not be limited to one people. Who will join in God's praise for what He has done?

Applying the Message

1. The psalmist was encouraged in his suffering by remembering that God had helped his ancestors in the past. We too may be encouraged by remembering the help that God has given to others and to us in the past. What examples of God's help to others or yourself are an encouragement to you?

2. Like David, we too may feel alone and forsaken. Enemies may surround us and seek our destruction. What can we do when we feel this way?

3. Verse 30 says "Posterity will serve Him; future generations will be told about the Lord." We are part of those future generations who have been told and now serve the Lord. Who can you tell about all that God has done for you through Christ?

Taking the Message Home

Review

Read Psalm 22 again, along with one or more of the passion accounts—John 19; Matthew 27:31–66; Luke 23:26–56; or Mark 15:15–47. Notice the parallels as this psalm vividly prophesies the suffering and death of Jesus Christ for us. Reflect on all that He has faced for us. We feel forsaken at times, but He was truly forsaken. We face opposition in life, but Jesus felt the entire world and even God opposed to Him as He suffered for our sin. We suffer as sinners, but He suffered in innocence. Thanks be to God for this wonderful gift!

Looking Ahead

Next time we will look at another messianic psalm—Psalm 110. Like Psalm 22, it vividly prophesies of Christ but not in His suffering—in His exalted glory.

Working Ahead

1. Read Psalm 110.

2. Who was Melchizedek? Read about him in a Bible dictionary. Also look at the article about priests in the Bible. What was the main job of a priest?

3. The Book of Hebrews has much to say about the meaning of Psalm 110. Read the following verses from Hebrews 4:14–5:10; 7:1–8:2; 9:11–14; 9:28; and 10:18.

Did You Know?

Psalm 22 is one of the most-quoted psalms in the New Testament. Here are some of the New Testament verses that quote this messianic psalm.

Verse:	Quoted in:
1	Matthew 27:46; Mark 15:34
7	Luke 23:35; Matthew 27:39; Mark 15:29
8	Matthew 27:43
15	John 19:28
16	Matthew 27:35; John 20:25
17	Luke 23:27, 35
18	Matthew 27:35; Mark 15:24; Luke 23:34; John 19:24
22	Hebrews 2:12
24	Hebrews 5:7
28	Matthew 6:13

Session 8

King, Priest, Messiah

Psalm 110

Approaching This Study

Psalm 110 is generally classified as a royal psalm, relating to events of Israel's monarchy. Many scholars think that this psalm was used at the coronation of a king. David, the author, may have written it for the coronation of his son, Solomon.

But that alone doesn't tell us all we need to know about this psalm. Some have called it "the most messianic psalm" because it is so frequently quoted in the New Testament. Jews before the coming of Christ viewed it as messianic. When Jesus questions the Pharisees about this view in Matthew 22, they do not object to His messianic use of the psalm. Jesus Himself then shows us how it applies to Him.

Only when we view this psalm in terms of the divine Messiah does a complete understanding open up for us.

An Overview

Psalm 110 is relatively short, but it is filled with insights about Christ. It can easily be divided into two sections:

The Messiah-King (verses 1–3)

The Messiah-Priest (verses 4–7)

Working with the Text

The Messiah-King (verses 1–3)

1. Read Psalm 110:1–3. The first verse is one of deep theological significance. David, who writes this palm, is king. As the king of Israel, who

is David's Lord? Does he have more than one Lord? Jesus challenged the Pharisees to explain this psalm. Does Jesus' question help us understand it's meaning? Read Matthew 22:41–46.

> While the Pharisees were gathered together, Jesus asked them, "What do you think about the Christ? Whose Son is He?" "The son of David," they replied. He said to them, "How is it then that David, speaking by the Spirit, calls Him 'Lord'? For he says, 'The Lord said to my Lord:
>
> 'Sit at My right hand
> until I put Your enemies
> under Your feet.'
>
> If then David calls him 'Lord,' how can He be His son?" No one could say a word in reply, and from that day on no one dared to ask Him any more questions. (Matthew 22:41–46)

2. This verse stumped the Pharisees. It cannot mean Solomon, the son of David who succeeded him as king, for David would not have called him Lord. Who can this verse refer to? How can He be David's son and David's Lord? See Matthew 1:1; Matthew 21:9; Revelation 22:16; and John 8:58. On the basis of this identity, what does Psalm 110:1 really mean?

> A record of the genealogy of Jesus Christ the son of David, the son of Abraham. (Matthew 1:1)

> The crowds that went ahead of Him and those that followed shouted, "Hosanna to the Son of David!"
> "Blessed is He who comes in the name of the Lord!"
> "Hosanna in the highest!" (Matthew 21:9)

> I, Jesus, have sent My angel to give you this testimony for the churches. I am the Root and the Offspring of David, and the bright Morning Star. (Revelation 22:16)

> "I tell you the truth," Jesus answered, "before Abraham was born, I am!" (John 8:58)

3. What "the Lord says to my Lord" is to sit at His right hand. What does this mean? Do we ever use similar language today? Read Matthew 26:64; Ephesians 1:20; Hebrews 8:1; and Matthew 28:18.

"Yes, it is as you say," Jesus replied. "But I say to all of you: In the future you will see the Son of Man sitting at the right hand of the Mighty One and coming on the clouds of heaven." (Matthew 26:64)

[God] raised Him from the dead and seated Him at His right hand in the heavenly realms. (Ephesians 1:20)

We do have such a high priest, who sat down at the right hand of the throne of the Majesty in heaven. (Hebrews 8:1)

Then Jesus came to them and said, "All authority in heaven and on earth has been given to Me." (Matthew 28:18)

4. According to verse 1, what will God make of the Messiah's enemies? What does this mean? How is this fulfilled by the Messiah? Read also Joshua 10:24; Malachi 4:3; Hebrews 2:8; and Ephesians 1:22.

When they had brought these kings to Joshua, he summoned all the men of Israel and said to the army commanders who had come with him, "Come here and put your feet on the necks of these kings." So they came forward and placed their feet on their necks. (Joshua 10:24)

"Then you will trample down the wicked; they will be ashes under the soles of your feet on the day when I do these things," says the LORD Almighty. (Malachi 4:3)

[God] put everything under His feet. In putting everything under Him, God left nothing that is not subject to Him. Yet at present we do not see everything subject to Him. (Hebrews 2:8)

God placed all things under His feet and appointed Him to be head over everything for the church. (Ephesians 1:22)

5. This section of Psalm 110 shows us that the Messiah will be a king. What does verse 2 say about His kingly reign? How is this fulfilled in Christ? See also Acts 1:8b.

You will be My witnesses in Jerusalem, and in all Judea and Samaria, and to the ends of the earth. (Acts 1:8b)

6. What does the first half of verse 3 mean? How does this apply to Christ?

7. The second half of verse 3 may be confusing. It is unclear whether it applies to the Messiah-King or to His willing soldiers. If it applies to the King, the verse means that He is clothed in majesty and that He is perpetually young. With each new day He receives the dew of His youth. If it applies to the willing soldiers, it means that there are as many young soldiers, clothed in majesty for battle, as there are dew drops in the morning. Luther applies this to the soldiers, paraphrasing, "After Thy victory Thy people will willingly make sacrifice to Thee in holy adornment. Thy children will be born to Thee like dew at the dawn of the morning" (*Luther's Works*, volume 13, p. 227). Which do you think is the most likely meaning? Does either option affect the meaning of the psalm?

The Messiah-Priest (verses 4–7)

1. Read Psalm 110:4–7. The psalm now changes topic and begins to consider the Messiah's office as priest. The priest's chief job was to offer sacrifices for the sins of the people. Jesus came to be the final sacrifice for the sins of the world. But there needs to be a priest to offer the sacrifice. Not just anyone could be a priest. What was a requirement for a priest according to Numbers 3:10? How did this present a theological problem for Jesus? See 1 Samuel 17:12a.

> Appoint Aaron and his sons to serve as priests; anyone else who approaches the sanctuary must be put to death. (Numbers 3:10)

> Now David was the son of an Ephrathite named Jesse, who was from Bethlehem in Judah. (1 Samuel 17:12a)

2. The solution to this problem is found in verse 4. The Messiah would be a priest according to the order of Melchizedek. Who was Melchizedek? When did he live? Why can the Messiah be a priest in the order of Melchizedek but not in the order of Aaron? See Genesis 14:18–20.

> Then Melchizedek king of Salem brought out bread and wine. He was priest of God Most High, and he blessed Abram, saying,

> "Blessed be Abram by God Most High,
> Creator of heaven and earth.
> And blessed be God Most High,
> who delivered your enemies into your hand."

> Then Abram gave Him a tenth of everything. (Genesis 14:18–20)

71

3. Verse 4, like verse 1, is considered an oracle, or direct word of prophecy from God. While the entire psalm is the Word of God, these words come to us in the form of a direct quote. While he gives us this Word of God, the psalmist also gives us a special reassurance about God's decrees. What does he say? Why is this reassuring? See also Malachi 3:6a and Hebrews 13:8.

I the LORD do not change. (Malachi 3:6a)

Jesus Christ is the same yesterday and today and forever. (Hebrews 13:8)

4. Verses 5–6 present us with an image of battle. With the Lord at his side, the king will be victorious in battle. We can easily see these verses applying to an earthly king. How do they apply to Christ also?

5. It might seem that verse 7 does not really fit into this section. Some interpreters consider this to be a description of the king who fights in battle. Finding a source of refreshment, he is able to continue in battle. Martin Luther took a different approach, applying this verse to Christ and showing the essence of His saving work. Christ does not come as a military leader but as the Savior. Read the accompanying "Martin Luther on Psalm 110." Does this interpretation help us to understand this entire section?

Martin Luther on Psalm 110

In this life, the prophet says, He will "drink from the brook"; that is, He will suffer and die. By "drink" or "cup" Scripture means any sort of torture, misery, and suffering, just as Christ prayed in the garden, where He sweat blood (Luke 22:44) and said (Matthew 26:39): "Dear Father, if it is possible, remove this cup from Me. But if it cannot be otherwise but that I drink it, Thy will be done." You see, that is the kind of drinking of which this verse speaks. …

Christ had to drink a "cup" on earth and be "drunk"; that is, He suffered torture and pain and perished before all the world. ... "He will drink from the brook" is intended to show that He will not feel ordinary or small pains and misery; but He will bear or endure the greatest, the most bitter and cruel pain and torture and will die a most contemptible death. ... "He will lift up His head" after He has drunk and suffered this. That is, He will become glorious and will reign over everything with power."

(From *Luther's Works*, volume 13, pp. 345–46. Copyright © 1956 by Concordia Publishing House. All rights reserved.)

Applying the Message

1. Most of this psalm focuses on the Messiah-Priest-King and not on His people. There are some verses that might seem to apply directly to people. Verse 3 speaks of the willing soldiers who fight in His army. Verses 1, 5, and 6 all speak of those who are opposed to Him. Which group do we fit in? What is the difference between these two groups?

2. This psalm speaks about God's power. He is at the right hand of God and will use His power in battle to accomplish victory. But how does He normally use His power? See Philippians 2:5–11, sometimes considered a New Testament psalm.

Your attitude should be the same as that of Christ Jesus:
Who, being in very nature God,
did not consider equality with God something to be grasped,
but made Himself nothing,
taking the very nature of a servant,
being made in human likeness.
And being found in appearance as a man,
He humbled Himself
and became obedient to death—

even death on a cross!
Therefore God exalted Him to the highest place
and gave Him the name that is above every name,
that at the name of Jesus every knee should bow,
in heaven and on earth and under the earth,
and every tongue confess that Jesus Christ is Lord,
to the glory of God the Father. (Philippians 2:5–12)

3. Jesus is King. In fact, He is "King of kings and Lord of lords" (Revelation 19:16). What makes His kingship a comfort to us?

Taking the Message Home

Review

Christ Jesus is our Messiah, King, and Priest as Psalm 110 declares. Reread this psalm and reflect on God's goodness in revealing these truths to His people even before the birth of Jesus. Also reread Philippians 2:5–12 and remember how Jesus used His power. How loving He is toward us!

Looking Ahead

Next time we will look at Psalm 84, a psalm that describes the wonders of God's temple and the even greater wonders of being in the presence of God.

Working Ahead

1. Read Psalm 84.

2. Read 1 Kings 6–7 or 1 Chronicles 3–4 for a description of Solomon's temple. What did it look like? What were its chief attractions?

Did You Know?

We've studied two psalms that are rightly classified as "messianic psalms" because they prophesy about the coming Messiah. There are many more prophesies of our Savior throughout the psalms. The following is a list of some of the verses from the psalms that are repeated in the New Testament at their fulfillment by Christ:

Psalm verse:	Fulfilled in:
You are my Son (Psalm 2:7)	Matthew 3:17
Nor will You let Your Holy One see decay (Psalm 16:10)	Acts 2:31; 13:15
They have pierced my hands and feet (Psalm 22:16)	John 20:25
They divide my garments among them and cast lots for my clothing (Psalm 22:18)	Matthew 27:35
He protects all his bones, not one of them will be broken (Psalm 34:20)	John 19:32–36
[They] gave me vinegar for my thirst (Psalm 69:21)	Matthew 27:34; John 19:29
The stone the builders rejected has become the capstone (Psalm 118:22)	Matthew 21:9
The LORD says to my Lord (Psalm 110:1)	Matthew 22:43–45; Acts 2:34–35; Hebrews 1:13
You are a priest forever (Psalm 110:4)	Hebrews 5:6; 7:17, 21

Session 9

The House of the Lord

Psalm 84

Approaching This Study

Psalm 84 focuses upon the house of God—the temple in Jerusalem. In His mercy, God had promised the people of Israel that He would be present in a specific place for their good. Because they knew where they could experience the presence of God, they knew where to go for forgiveness, to hear His truth, and to pray. Of course God can do anything He wants. He is present in all places and is not confined to a building. But God promised that in this place He would be present for their good. They knew where to go.

The writer of Psalm 84 realizes the temple is the house of God. Naturally he longs to be there. He longs to live in the presence of God forever. His thoughts overflow in this psalm. The temple is a beautiful place, and those who live there are blessed. I want to be there! But even if he is not in the temple, he knows that he is blessed by God.

We, too, have experienced the presence of God and His many blessings. Because He has so freely blessed us in Jesus Christ, we praise Him and in faith cry out like the psalmist, "O LORD Almighty, blessed is the man who trusts in You."

An Overview

The entire psalm focuses on the dwelling place of God. The psalm envisions the temple itself, those who live in it, those who travel to it, and the king whose palace is nearby. Throughout the psalm, we see the desire of the psalmist to make this place his own home. The following outlines the psalm's structure:

Working with the Text

An Introduction to Psalm 84

The introduction of Psalm 84 tells us two basic pieces of information. This is a psalm "according to gittith" and "of the Sons of Korah." Gittith is a Hebrew word that we find at the beginning of Psalm 8, 81, and 84. We do not know the precise meaning of this word. Biblical scholars generally suggest three possibilities: (1) it may be a particular instrument that was to accompany the psalm; (2) it may be a musical mode; or (3) it might be the name of a melody to which it should be sung.

"The Sons of Korah" are generally considered to have been a musical guild who were of the tribe of Levi. We read of them singing in 2 Chronicles 20:19. A number of psalms share this same ascription, "of the Sons of Korah," including Psalms 42, 44–49, 84–85, and 87–88.

Longing for God and His Temple (verses 1–2)

1. Read Psalm 84:1–2. The psalmist says that God's dwelling place is lovely. Old Testament believers knew that God was not confined to the temple (1 Kings 8:27), but they also knew that God had promised to dwell in the temple. They would find Him there. But access to the temple was limited. Gentiles could only go to a certain court. There was a limit to how far a woman could go into the building. All but priests were restricted from the holy place, and only the high priest could enter the most holy place—and that only once a year on the day of atonement. Because of this, the psalmist could not have seen the temple in its entirety. If he doesn't have access to the whole temple, how can he say that the place of God's dwelling is lovely?

> But will God really dwell on earth? The heavens, even the highest heaven, cannot contain You. How much less this temple I have built! (1 Kings 8:27)

2. The psalmist shows us in these verses that there are two things he longs to see. What are they? How do these verses show that this desire fills his entire life?

Blessings of the Temple Inhabitants (verses 3–4)

1. Read verses 3–4. What does the psalm say about birds? What does this tell us about God? See also Matthew 6:26. Why do you think the psalmist uses this image?

> Look at the birds of the air; they do not sow or reap or store away in barns, and yet your heavenly Father feeds them. Are you not much more valuable than they? (Matthew 6:26)

2. After using the illustration of birds, the psalm switches to speak of people who are blessed. Who are they? Why are they blessed?

Blessings of the Pilgrims (verses 5–7)

1. Read verses 5–7. In the previous verse we read that those who dwell in God's house are blessed. Now we see that God's blessing is expanded to those outside the temple. Those whose hearts are set on pilgrimages are blessed. These are people who travel to the temple, and they are aided in their journey by God Himself. What is it that upholds them according to verses 5 and 7? May we be upheld by the same thing? See also Psalm 81:1; Philippians 4:13; and Isaiah 40:31.

Sing for joy to God our strength;
shout aloud to the God of Jacob! (Psalm 81:1)

I can do everything through Him who gives me strength. (Philippians 4:13)

But those who hope in the LORD
will renew their strength.
They will soar on wings like eagles;
they will run and not grow weary,
they will walk and not be faint. (Isaiah 40:31)

2. Verse 6 tells us that the pilgrims have an effect on the world around them. "Baca" means "balsam tree"—a tree that grows in a dry environment. It is very similar to a Hebrew word for "weeping." So Martin Luther translates "Valley of Baca" as "vale of sorrow." In either sense, the point is the same. When the pilgrims pass through a difficult place, God is able to transform it for them. What happens to this place, and how does it happen?

Prayer for the King (verses 8–9)

Read verses 8–9. God's temple is in Jerusalem. As they travel to the temple, the pilgrims see the royal palace and say these verses as a prayer for the king. How do these verses describe the king? What does he do for his subjects? What are their responsibilities to their king? See also verse 11; 1 Timothy 2:1–2; and Romans 13:1.

I urge, then, first of all, that requests, prayers, intercession and thanksgiving be made for everyone—for kings and all those in authority, that we may live peaceful and quiet lives in all godliness and holiness. (1 Timothy 2:1–2)

Everyone must submit himself to the governing authorities, for there is no authority except that which God has established. The authorities that exist have been established by God. (Romans 13:1)

Longing to Live in God's House (verses 10–12)

1. Read verses 10–12. Note the contrasts in verse 10. What does the psalmist say that goes against the normal pattern of the world? Why is he able to say these things? See also Psalm 27:4.

One thing I ask of the LORD,
this is what I seek:
that I may dwell in the house of the LORD
all the days of my life,
to gaze upon the beauty of the LORD
and to seek Him in His temple. (Psalm 27:4)

2. Verse 11 shows the blessings that the Lord gives. How does the psalmist describe God? What motivates our Lord to do these things for us? See also 1 Peter 5:7.

Cast all your anxiety on Him because He cares for you. (1 Peter 5:7)

3. Verse 12 refers to someone God has blessed. We saw the same claim made two other times in this psalm (verses 4–5). Considering these verses, what makes us truly blessed?

Applying the Message

1. This psalm shows the overwhelming desire of the author to come to God's house. He wishes that he was constantly in the temple and notes that those who are in the temple are truly blessed. Do we have the same desire to be in the Lord's house? How might we have the same zeal for God's presence and worship as the psalmist?

2. As the pilgrim travels to the temple, the Valley of Baca becomes a place of springs. The pilgrimage transforms the pilgrim's world. As we pass through this life we may have an impact on the world around us. What might be transformed by God's power in our life, home, church, community, or world?

3. Verse 11 says that God withholds no good thing from those whose walk is blameless. Does this verse apply to us? Does God really withhold nothing good from us?

4. Verse 12 summarizes the psalm and brings it to a conclusion:

"Blessed is the man who trusts in You." Are we blessed? What does it mean to trust God?

Taking the Message Home

Review

Throughout the week, reflect on God's amazing blessings to us. Though we could never deserve His goodness, He continues to care for us, His children.

Read Psalm 84 again. Compare it to Psalm 63, which contains similar ideas. Does Psalm 63 help you understand Psalm 84 better?

As Psalm 84 includes a prayer for the king, in your prayers this week, take the time to pray for our government and its leaders.

Looking Ahead

Next time we will study one of the most challenging psalms in the entire book—Psalm 137. This is one of the "imprecatory" psalms, or psalms of cursing. Through it we will wrestle with the challenging topic of human suffering.

Working Ahead

1. Read Psalm 137.

2. To provide context for Psalm 137, read 2 Kings 25:1–26, an account of the conquering of Jerusalem. Psalm 137 is a response to these events.

3. Find Babylon and Edom in a Bible atlas or on a map in your Bible.

Did You Know?

It is well known that the longest chapter of the Bible is Psalm 119. Its 176 verses easily eclipse the length of all the other chapters. But not many people know that Psalm 117 is the shortest psalm—and at only 2 verses it is also the shortest chapter in the Bible. Joining these two extremes together is Psalm 118, which holds the distinction of being the middle chapter of the Bible.

Session 10

The Horror of Exile

Psalm 137

Approaching This Study

Several times in their history, God's people were taken against their will by invading countries into exile. In the sixth century B.C., many people were carried away to Babylon after enduring military defeat. This would be a hardship for any person, but for Abraham's descendants, to whom God had promised their own land as an eternal inheritance, it was inconceivable. Their army was defeated; Jerusalem, the city of God, was conquered. Pagans stole their possessions and murdered their families.

In Babylon they were humiliated. Some of their captors tormented them, mocking God and His people. Their captors tried to coerce these homesick Israelites to adapt to their ways and to reject the God of Abraham, Isaac, and Jacob.

Psalm 137 was written in the context of suffering. It is a poignant song of suffering but also of shocking anger. The psalmist yearns for his homeland and then calls down curses upon his captors. Thus, the psalm is classified as an "imprecatory" psalm—a psalm that calls for God's judgment on one's enemies. In studying the words of the psalmist, we learn more of God's response to human suffering.

An Overview

The lament of Psalm 137 addresses three different themes:

Longing for Home with a Crushed Spirit (Verses 1–4)

A Warning to the Psalmist (Verses 5–6)

A Curse for the Captors (Verses 7–9)

Working with the Text

Longing for Home with a Crushed Spirit (verses 1–4)

1. Read Psalm 137:1–4. As the psalm opens, the speaker is "by the rivers of Babylon." The Tigris and the Euphrates rivers flowed through Babylon. Beside these waters the psalmist weeps. What causes his sorrow? Why do you think he mentions his sorrow and the rivers in the same verse? See also Acts 16:13, which describes the Jewish community in the city of Philippi.

> On the Sabbath we went outside the city gate to the river, where we expected to find a place of prayer. We sat down and began to speak to the women who had gathered there. (Acts 16:13)

2. The psalm gives other reasons for the psalmist's sorrow. His captors torment him, demanding that he sing songs for them. They are not asking merely for music. They have heard of the music of the Jews and demand that it be sung for their entertainment. What are the "songs of Zion"? Perhaps the captors want to mock their prisoners because of the content of the psalms (see also Psalm 79:10a), or perhaps they simply want to be entertained. Why are both of these demeaning uses of the Jews' music?

> Why should the nations say,
> "Where is their God?" (Psalm 79:10a)

3. How does the psalmist respond to the Babylonian request? How does this reflect not only the despair of the moment but also hope for the future?

A Warning to the Psalmist (verses 5–6)

1. Read verses 5–6. The tone of the psalm now begins to change from contemplative sadness to an outward reaction to horrible events. In these verses, the psalmist contrasts remembering and forgetting. Note the distinction between "remember" and "forget" as used in these verses and in verses 1 and 7. Who is remembering and forgetting? What is it that is remembered and forgotten? Whose memory is the strongest? See also Luke 23:42–43.

> Then he said, "Jesus, remember me when You come into Your kingdom." Jesus answered him, "I tell you the truth, today you will be with Me in paradise." (Luke 23:42–43)

2. Many people are shocked by the harsh words of this psalm in verses 7–9. We must be careful not to read these verses out of context. Before he speaks his request for judgment, the psalmist addresses himself. What warning does he issue to himself? Why is it important that we understand these words before reading his words against Israel's enemies?

3. The focus of this section and the psalmist's memory is Jerusalem (or Zion). Why is this city important? See also Psalm 2:6 and Psalm 46:4.

> I have installed My King
> on Zion, My holy hill. (Psalm 2:6)

> There is a river whose streams make glad the city of God,
> The holy place where the Most High dwells. (Psalm 46:4)

A Curse for the Captors (verses 7–9)

1. Read verses 7–9. The psalmist first directs his anger against the Edomites. While the Edomites were not the psalmist's captors, what had they done to God's people? See also Joel 3:19 and Obadiah 8, 10–11, 15b. What does the psalmist ask of God regarding the Edomites?

> Egypt will be desolate,
> Edom a desert waste,
> because of the violence done to the people of Judah,
> in whose land they shed innocent blood. (Joel 3:19)

> "In that day," declares the LORD,
> "will I not destroy the wise men of Edom,
> men of understanding in the mountains of Esau?" ...
> Because of the violence against your brother Jacob,
> you will be covered with shame;
> you will be destroyed forever.
> On the day you stood aloof
> while strangers carried off his wealth
> and foreigners entered his gates
> and cast lots for Jerusalem,
> you were like one of them. ...
> As you have done, it will be done to you;
> your deeds will return upon your own head. (Obadiah 8, 10–11, 15b)

2. Next the psalmist turns to the Jews' captors—the Babylonians. Summarize what you learned about the Babylonians from 2 Kings 25:1–26. What had they done to Jerusalem and its inhabitants? What is the fate of Babylon?

3. Without a doubt, the most difficult verse of this psalm is verse 9. We might understand the psalmist's call for God's judgment against the Babylonian army, but it is difficult for us to comprehend the words directed against their infants. Violence against infants was not uncommon in the ancient world and is found in other sections of the Old Testament as well (for example, see Nahum 3:10). What could motivate the psalmist to say such a thing? Do you think he means these words literally or figuratively? Who carries out this wish?

> Yet she was taken captive
> and went into exile.
> Her infants were dashed to pieces
> at the head of every street.
> Lots were cast for her nobles,
> and all her great men were put in chains. (Nahum 3:10)

Applying the Message

1. The psalmist refused the demands of his captors for a song, saying, "How can we sing the songs of the LORD while in a foreign land?" His refusal was directly related to the fact that God's temple was in Jerusalem. Today there is no temple in Jerusalem, and we live in a "foreign land." Where may the Lord's songs be sung today? See John 4:21, 23–24 and Revelation 21:22.

> Jesus declared, "Believe Me, woman, a time is coming when you will worship the Father neither on this mountain nor in Jerusalem. … A time is coming and has now come when the true worshipers will worship the Father in spirit and truth, for they are the kind of worshipers the Father seeks. God is spirit, and His worshipers must worship in spirit and in truth." (John 4:21, 23–24)

> I did not see a temple in the city, because the Lord God Almighty and the Lamb are its temple. (Revelation 21:22)

2. A Christian reading this psalm will likely struggle with the attitude of the psalmist in verses 7–9. How can he ask God to do these terrible things? Does not God call us to forgive? See Mark 11:25; Luke 23:34; and Matthew 18:21–22. Why do you think God has allowed these challenging words to remain a part of Scripture? We might better understand the words of this psalm if we understand the depth of the psalmist's suffering. What events in modern times might cause people to say similar words?

> And when you stand praying, if you hold anything against anyone, forgive him, so that your Father in heaven may forgive you your sins. (Mark 11:25–26)

> Jesus said, "Father, forgive them, for they do not know what they are doing." (Luke 23:34)

> Then Peter came to Jesus and asked, "Lord, how many times shall I forgive my brother when he sins against me? Up to seven times?" Jesus answered, "I tell you, not seven times, but seventy-seven times." (Matthew 18:21–22)

3. While the psalm writer had been victimized by his captors and had called for their judgment, he did not carry this judgment out himself. Why didn't he seek revenge personally? See Romans 12:19b and Jeremiah 11:20. When will the judgment he seeks ultimately occur? How might we apply this in our life?

> "It is Mine to avenge; I will repay," says the Lord. (Romans 12:19b)

> But, O LORD Almighty, You who judge righteously
> and test the heart and mind,
> let me see Your vengeance upon them,
> for to You I have committed my cause. (Jeremiah 11:20)

4. Psalm 137 allows us to examine a human response to suffering. Dealing with pain and suffering is difficult for all people, but we all must face suffering at some point in our life. What may we learn from this psalm that will help us deal with suffering?

Taking the Message Home

Review

For a more extended treatment of the grief of exile, read Lamentations 1–2. Note similarities and differences with Psalm 137.

This study looked at a psalm about exile. By God's grace, the exile had an end. Browse through the book of Ezra or Nehemiah and see some of the things that the exiles did on their return home.

Looking Ahead

Next time we will study Psalm 46. While Psalm 137 responds to the destruction of Jerusalem and the captivity of God's people, Psalm 46 considers a time when God delivered Jerusalem from attackers.

Working Ahead

1. Read Psalm 46.

2. Read 2 Kings 18:13–19:36. This passage tells the story of the miraculous deliverance of God's people from the Assyrians. This is the likely context for the praise of God we find in Psalm 46.

3. Who were the Assyrians? Look this up in a Bible dictionary.

Did You Know?

Melodies of the Psalms

The information at the beginning of some psalms (the superscription) tells us a number of things about the psalm: who wrote it; what the occasion was; the desired instruments or use; and sometimes the melody that the author had in mind. Some of the more notable melodies and the psalm(s) they are connected with include

Melody Name	Psalms
Do Not Destroy (possibly a song of the vineyards)	57–59, 75
Doe of the Morning	22
The Dove on the Distant Oaks	56
Gittith (possibly a song of the winepresses)	8, 81, 84
Lilies	45, 69, 80
Mahalath or Mahalath Leannoth (possibly a sad melody)	53, 88
Muth-labben (possibly a song about the death of a son)	9

Session 11

A Strong Fortress

Psalm 46

Approaching This Study

During the reign of King Hezekiah, the Assyrian king, Sennacherib captured many cities in Judah. Hezekiah paid a ransom for the cities with gold and silver from the Lord's temple and from his palace. Sennacherib was not satisfied. Instead, he sent his armies to capture Jerusalem.

Hezekiah went into the temple of the Lord in great anguish. Earnestly he prayed to the Lord for deliverance. Knowing that his king was seeking God's guidance, the prophet Isaiah went to him and comforted Hezekiah, foretelling that Sennacharib would return to Assyria, where he would die.

That night, the angel of the Lord entered the Assyrian camp and killed 185,000 soldiers. Defeated before the battle had begun, Sennacharib returned to Assyria, where he himself was killed. So God's people were victorious without having to fight the battle. In response to God's action, they sang the song that we know as Psalm 46.

An Overview

This psalm celebrates God's protection of His people and His deliverance. He is a strong fortress for His people. The psalm can be divided into three sections:

God Is Stronger than Nature (verses 1–3)

God Protects Jerusalem with His Power (verses 4–7)

God Is Stronger than All Enemies (verses 8–11)

Working with the Text

God Is Stronger than Nature (verses 1–3)

Alamoth

The superscription of Psalm 46 says it is a song "according to alamoth." The meaning of this word is unclear. It probably derives from the Hebrew word for "young women" and so in a musical context may mean "for soprano voices." 1 Chronicles 15:20 demonstrates that it is a musical term, mentioning that certain people "were to play the lyres according to alamoth."

1. Read Psalm 46:1–3. The first verse declares three things about God. Each of them provides information about a different aspect of God's nature. What do they tell us about God? Why do you think the psalmist chose these words to describe God?

2. Verses 2 and 3 describe terrible events in nature. The image is actually a reversal of God's creating work. See Genesis 1:9–10 and Jeremiah 5:22. The psalm does not say that these events will occur but rather uses them to show that "even if these things happen …" How would most people react to events like these? What is the surprising reaction of the people of God? Why can His people view such terrifying events in this way?

> And God said, "Let the water under the sky be gathered to one place, and let dry ground appear." And it was so. God called the dry ground "land," and the gathered waters He called "seas." And God saw that it was good. (Genesis 1:9–10)

> "Should you not fear Me?" declares the LORD.
> "Should you not tremble in My presence?
> I made the sand a boundary for the sea,
> an everlasting barrier it cannot cross.
> The waves may roll, but they cannot prevail;
> they may roar, but they cannot cross it." (Jeremiah 5:22)

God Protects Jerusalem with His Power (verses 4–7)

1. Read verses 4–7. From the destructive power of the seas we now look at a sustaining stream. When a city was under attack by an opposing army, the one thing they desperately needed was a source of water. Without water they would soon have to surrender. At the time this psalm was written, Jerusalem had a protected water supply that helped to sustain their lives. But the psalm doesn't really seem to be talking about this water. Look at the two parallel thoughts in verse 4. What is the meaning of the water? How is this a good description?

2. The theme of the sustaining river is present throughout Holy Scripture. With Psalm 46 in mind, read Genesis 2:10; John 4:13–14; and Revelation 22:1–2. What do these verses reveal about the river image?

A river watering the garden flowed from Eden; from there it was separated into four headwaters. (Genesis 2:10)

Jesus answered, "Everyone who drinks this water will be thirsty again, but whoever drinks the water I give him will never thirst. Indeed, the water I give him will become in him a spring of water welling up to eternal life." (John 4:13–14)

Then the angel showed me the river of the water of life, as clear as crystal, flowing from the throne of God and of the Lamb down the middle of the great street of the city. (Revelation 22:1–2a)

3. The people of God, then and now, are able to withstand the attacks of nature and of other nations because God is their refuge and strength. How does verse 5 emphasize this point? See also Isaiah 12:6; Matthew 1:23; and Revelation 21:3.

Shout aloud and sing for joy, people of Zion,
for great is the Holy One of Israel among you. (Isaiah 12:6)

The virgin will be with child and will give birth to a son, and they will call Him Immanuel—which means, "God with us." (Matthew 1:23)

And I heard a loud voice from the throne saying, "Now the dwelling of God is with men, and He will live with them. They will be His people, and God Himself will be with them and be their God." (Revelation 21:3)

4. Verse 6 describes God's supremacy not only over creation but also over all nations. How is God's wrath unleashed on the nations who oppose Him? How is their destruction pictured? When did (or will) this happen? See also Micah 1:4.

The mountains melt beneath Him
and the valleys split apart,
like wax before the fire,
like water rushing down a slope. (Micah 1:4)

5. This section reveals the amazing power of God over the earth and all nations. Yet He does not destroy His people. Instead, He lovingly cares for them. When does the psalmist specifically say that God will help His people? Why do you think he uses this wording?

God Is Stronger than All Enemies (verses 8–11)

1. Read verses 8–11. The psalm has described God's strength and protection, telling the people what God would do. In these verses the psalmist describes what God has already accomplished for His people. What has God done(vv. 8–9)?

2. The people are told to see the works of the Lord. God has worked on their behalf. What does God ask of His people in exchange? How are they to respond?

3. Verses 7 and 11 serve as an antiphon or refrain for the psalm. They are similar to verse 1. How do these words help to summarize and focus the message of the psalm? What is the attitude behind these verses? See also Romans 8:31.

> What, then, shall we say in response to this? If God is for us, who can be against us? (Romans 8:31)

Applying the Message

1. The powerful words of praise that this psalm contains testify to the faithfulness of God towards His people. At times of great crisis, the Israelites learned to rely on the strength, help, and protection of the God who loved them. God's faithfulness hasn't changed. How do we need Him as our refuge and strength today? From what do we need protection? What do we fear?

2. The psalmist invited God's people to come and see His works. They saw that He had defeated their enemies, and they rejoiced in His gifts. Today we are invited to come and see the works of the Lord. What can we show and tell others to demonstrate God's amazing power?

3. In verse 10, God says, "Be still and know that I am God." God is in control and uses His power on our behalf. When is this verse particularly comforting to you? When do we need to remember to "be still"? See also Philippians 4:6–7.

> Do not be anxious about anything, but in everything, by prayer and petition, with thanksgiving, present your requests to God. And the peace of God, which transcends all understanding, will guard your hearts and your minds in Christ Jesus. (Philippians 4:6–7)

Taking the Message Home

Review

Psalm 46 strongly moved Martin Luther. This psalm became the best-known hymn he wrote, "A Mighty Fortress Is Our God." Read Psalm 46 and "A Mighty Fortress" and see how Luther applied this psalm to our entire Christian life.

Psalms 46–48 all offer praises to God for the temple and for His city, Jerusalem. Read all three of these psalms and note their similarities.

Looking Ahead

Next time we will study our final psalm—Psalm 136. It is a psalm of praise that gives thanks to God for many different things that He did for His people. We will join our praise with the psalmist to give thanks to our God for His everlasting love and mercy.

Working Ahead

1. Read Psalm 136.

2. This psalm refers to many different events from Israel's history. For the background of some of them, browse through the Book of Exodus, chapters 11–15, and notice what happens there.

3. Review the story of God's creation in Genesis 1:1–2:3. How does this motivate us to thank and praise our God?

Did You Know?

The King James Bible was translated in 1611. While we do not know everyone who was involved in this translation, many people have wondered if William Shakespeare may have been involved. A strange analysis notes that in 1611, Shakespeare was 46 years old. The 46th word from the beginning of Psalm 46 is "shake." The 46th word from the end is "spear." Some people think that Shakespeare worked on this psalm, and in honor of his 46th birthday, slipped his name into the psalm.

Session 12

God's Eternal Love

Psalm 136

Approaching This Study

During the last 11 sessions we have examined a wide variety of psalms. We have learned how to read the psalms. We have confessed God's goodness and we have confessed our sin. We have praised the God of all creation, who also cares for us in our day-to-day life. We have heard vivid prophecies of our Savior and have sung of His tender care for us. What riches the psalms have for us!

Our final psalm is a psalm of praise. Psalm 136 is sometimes referred to as the "Great Hallel." Hallel means praise (the Hebrew word "Halleluia" means "Praise to Yahweh"). A number of psalms are classified as hallel psalms, but this one is the Great Hallel. As we read its words we quickly see how it got this name.

This psalm is notable for its repeating refrain at the end of each verse. Most scholars believe that the psalm was designed to be sung antiphonally—a choir or soloist would sing the verse, and the congregation would join in the refrain "His love endures forever."

An Overview

In calling us to praise and thank God, the psalm considers many specific works of God for which we should thank Him. We see these as

A Call to Praise (verses 1–3)

Praise the Creator (verses 4–9)

Praise the Deliverer (verses 10–16)

Praise the Conqueror (verses 17–22)

Praise the God of All (verses 23–26)

Working with the Text

A Call to Praise (verses 1–3)

1. Read Psalm 136:1–3. We find the words of verse 1 in a number of other Bible passages. They also are repeated in the worship of the church and in prayer. The second half of the verse, "His love endures forever," forms the refrain of this psalm and is repeated in every verse. What is the meaning of this phrase? Look at a number of Bible translations to see how this verse is translated in different ways.

2. Verses 2 and 3 revel in God's supremacy over all others. What words does the psalmist use to show that there is no being like God? See also Deuteronomy 10:17 and Revelation 17:14. What do these words imply?

> For the LORD your God is God of gods and Lord of lords, the great God, mighty and awesome, who shows no partiality and accepts no bribes. (Deuteronomy 10:17)

> They will make war against the Lamb, but the Lamb will overcome them because He is Lord of lords and King of kings—and with Him will be His called, chosen and faithful followers. (Revelation 17:14)

3. What does verse 1 give as a motivation for our thanks to God? What evidence of this do we see in the world and in our own life? See also Matthew 19:17a and Psalm 145:9.

> "Why do you ask Me about what is good?" Jesus replied. "There is only One who is good." (Matthew 19:17a)

> The LORD is good to all;
> He has compassion on all He has made. (Psalm 145:9)

Praise the Creator (verses 4–9)

1. Read verses 4–9. Here the psalm calls us to thank God because of His creative work. You may want to compare these verses with Genesis 1:1–19. These verses focus on part of God's creation. What part is highlighted? What part do these verses leave out? How does the focus of these verses help us to see more reasons to praise God?

2. While many people today want to debate endlessly the origin of the universe, Psalm 136 is very plain in its assertions. How does the psalmist assert that God created the universe? What is his reason for reminding us of these truths? See also Job 38:4–7.

> Where were you when I laid the earth's foundation?
> Tell me, if you understand.
> Who marked off its dimensions? Surely you know!
> Who stretched a measuring line across it?
> On what were its footings set,
> or who laid its cornerstone—
> while the morning stars sang together
> and all the angels shouted for joy? (Job 38:4–7)

Praise the Deliverer (verses 10–16)

1. Read verses 10–16. In these verses, three aspects of God's deliverance of His people, Israel, in the Exodus from Egypt are seen as motivation for thanks. The first is the Passover and the release from Egypt

(verses 10–12). What happened on that night? See also Exodus 12:22–23, 29–32. Why are these terrifying events reason for the psalmist to praise God? Do they give us reason to praise God as well? See 1 Corinthians 5:7b.

> Take a bunch of hyssop, dip it into the blood in the basin and put some of the blood on the top and on both sides of the doorframe. Not one of you shall go out the door of his house until morning. When the LORD goes through the land to strike down the Egyptians, He will see the blood on the top and sides of the doorframe and will pass over that doorway, and He will not permit the destroyer to enter your houses and strike you down. …

> At midnight the LORD struck down all the firstborn in Egypt, from the firstborn of Pharaoh, who sat on the throne, to the firstborn of the prisoner, who was in the dungeon, and the firstborn of all the livestock as well. Pharaoh and all his officials and all the Egyptians got up during the night, and there was loud wailing in Egypt, for there was not a house without someone dead. During the night Pharaoh summoned Moses and Aaron and said, "Up! Leave my people, you and the Israelites! Go, worship the LORD as you have requested." (Exodus 12:22–23; 29–31)

> For Christ, our Passover lamb, has been sacrificed. (1 Corinthians 5:7b)

2. The second facet of the Exodus that the psalm uses as a motivation for praise is the miraculous crossing of the Red Sea. Again, this event was a blessing for the faithful but horrible for God's enemies. Look over the events at the Red Sea in Exodus 14:21–22, 27–29 and in Hebrews 11:29. How did God manifest His power on that day? How does this motivate us to praise God? Have we experienced similar miracles in our life? See Romans 6:3–4.

> Then Moses stretched out his hand over the sea, and all that night the LORD drove the sea back with a strong east wind and turned it into dry land. The waters were divided, and the Israelites went through the sea on dry ground, with a wall of water on their right and on their left. …

Moses stretched out his hand over the sea, and at daybreak the sea went back to its place. The Egyptians were fleeing toward it, and the LORD swept them into the sea. The water flowed back and covered the chariots and horsemen—the entire army of Pharaoh that had followed the Israelites into the sea. Not one of them survived. But the Israelites went through the sea on dry ground, with a wall of water on their right and on their left. (Exodus 14:21–22, 27–29)

By faith the people passed through the Red Sea as on dry land; but when the Egyptians tried to do so, they were drowned. (Hebrews 11:29)

Don't you know that all of us who were baptized into Christ Jesus were baptized into His death? We were therefore buried with Him through baptism into death in order that, just as Christ was raised from the dead through the glory of the Father, we too may live a new life. (Romans 6:3–4)

3. The third aspect of the Exodus that this psalm uses to motivate our praise is God's gracious action of leading His people through the wilderness (verse 16). After being freed from slavery, Israel chose slavery to sin, rebelling against God. Because of this rebellion, their entry into the Promised Land was delayed for 40 years. But even then God did not leave them alone. Instead, He continued to lead them. What were some of the things that God did for Israel in these years? See Deuteronomy 8:15–16. Does God do similar things for us?

He led you through the vast and dreadful desert, that thirsty and waterless land, with its venomous snakes and scorpions. He brought you water out of hard rock. He gave you manna to eat in the desert, something your fathers had never known, to humble and to test you so that in the end it might go well with you. (Deuteronomy 8:15–16)

Praise the Conqueror (verses 17–22)

1. Read verses 17–22. At the end of the Exodus, God's people crossed into the Promised Land. Even then, God did not leave them alone. The Lord went before them and gave the land into their hands. What in these verses demonstrates to us that God did the work rather than the Israelites? Apply this fact to your life. See Hebrews 9:15.

> For this reason Christ is the mediator of a new covenant, that those who are called may receive the promised eternal inheritance—now that He has died as a ransom to set them free from the sins committed under the first covenant. (Hebrews 9:15)

2. Verses 19 and 20 speak specifically about two of the kings who opposed Israel and were defeated. Who were Sihon and Og? How were they defeated in battle? See Numbers 21:21–24, 33–35.

> Israel sent messengers to say to Sihon king of the Amorites:

> "Let us pass through your country. We will not turn aside into any field or vineyard, or drink water from any well. We will travel along the king's highway until we have passed through your territory."

> But Sihon would not let Israel pass through his territory. He mustered his entire army and marched out into the desert against Israel. When he reached Jahaz, he fought with Israel. Israel, however, put him to the sword and took over his land from the Arnon to the Jabbok, but only as far as the Ammonites, because their border was fortified. (Numbers 21:21–24)

> Then they turned and went up along the road toward Bashan, and Og king of Bashan and his whole army marched out to meet them in battle at Edrei.

> The LORD said to Moses, "Do not be afraid of him, for I have handed him over to you, with his whole army and his land. Do to him what you did to Sihon king of the Amorites, who reigned in Heshbon."

So they struck him down, together with his sons and his whole army, leaving them no survivors. And they took possession of his land. (Numbers 21:33–35)

Praise the God of All (verses 23–26)

1. Read verses 23–26. We might be tempted to assume that Psalm 136:10–22 was only about one nation—Israel. What in these verses makes it clear that God is not the God of one nation alone but of all creation?

2. Verse 25 tells us that one reason we praise God is that He gives food to all creatures. See also Psalm 145:15. How does this demonstrate God's care for us? See also Matthew 6:26.

The eyes of all look to You,
and You give them their food at the proper time. (Psalm 145:15)

Look at the birds of the air; they do not sow or reap or store away in barns, and yet your heavenly Father feeds them. Are you not much more valuable than they? (Matthew 6:26)

3. Every verse of Psalm 136 ends with the same words: "His love endures forever." The psalmist gives many different reasons for us to give thanks to God. How does the psalm, as a whole, motivate us to praise God?

Applying the Message

1. A number of the reasons to thank God that the psalmist provides are not pleasant to everyone. Some of the things for which the psalmist praises God involve hardships endured by people. Look through the psalm again and identify these things. What does this tell us about our relationship with God and with other people? Was it really necessary that others suffer these misfortunes? Why?

2. Look over the psalm again and notice all the reasons that we have to give thanks to God. If we were writing the psalm today, our list would probably include different reasons to give thanks to God. What would you include in this psalm if you wrote it today?

Taking the Message Home

Review

Read Psalm 135 and compare it to Psalm 136. Notice the similarities between the psalms (but without the refrain). Continue to think of things that you might include in your own psalm. Thank God for all of His goodness.

Look back over the psalms that we have studied. Notice the different character and tone of these psalms. They come from a wide variety of circumstances and contexts, but all of them help us see God's action in our life.

We've only looked at 12 psalms out of 150. Resolve to read the psalms as a regular part of your personal devotions.

Did You Know?

Many Christians have found great blessings in a regular reading of the psalms. A number of systems have been developed to help people remember to read through the psalms on a regular basis. Some even make a habit of reading through the entire book every month. While the details vary, the basic principle is simple: read five or six psalms every day (Psalm 119 counts as a full day's reading by itself), and you will complete the entire psalter (150 psalms in all) within a month. It doesn't take very long, but the rewards are worth it!

Glossary

adultery. Consensual sexual intercourse between a person and another person's spouse. Jesus interprets the Sixth Commandment (which forbids adultery) as forbidding all kinds of sexual indecency in both deed and thought (Matthew 5:28).

amen. The word *amen* is spoken when one wants to express "so be it." It indicates confirmation or agreement.

angels. Literally "messengers." Most often used to refer to spiritual, heavenly beings who were created by God. Some angels, led by Satan, rebelled against God. Holy angels, who did not rebel, continually do God's bidding. They protect and serve people who have faith in God. Angels differ in rank.

anoint. To apply oil to a person or thing. Sometimes anointing was simply a part of grooming. After washing or bathing, people anointed themselves. Hosts anointed their guests as an act of courtesy or respect. Anointing was also done at a person's induction into the office of priest, king, or sometimes prophet to indicate that the person was being set apart for that particular service. Christ was anointed with the Holy Spirit.

Antichrist. One who is both an enemy of Christ and a usurper of His rights and names.

apocalyptic literature. A type of literature that is highly symbolic and deals with the revelation of mysteries, especially concerning the end times. Biblical examples of this type of literature include Daniel 7–12 and Revelation. Apocalyptic literature, usually written in times of oppression, was primarily meant to encourage God's people.

apostles. Used several times in a general sense to mean "messengers," in the New Testament this word most often refers to those who were specifically commissioned by Jesus to proclaim the Gospel. Most prominent of the apostles were the Twelve and Paul. The teaching of the apostles, along with that of the prophets, is the foundation of the church. *See also* disciples.

Baptism. Christian Baptism—the application of water in the name of the triune God (Father, Son, and Holy Spirit) is a sacrament. The way the water is applied to the individual can vary. The New Testament makes no distinction between adult and infant Baptism. Christian Baptism works the forgiveness of sins; it delivers one from spiritual death and the devil; it gives eternal salvation to all who believe in Christ; it confers the Holy Spirit. Baptism also makes one a member of the body of Christ, the church. *See also* sacrament.

Bethlehem. The birthplace of Jesus Christ, thus fulfilling the Old Testament prophecy found in Micah 5:2.

Capernaum. The center of Jesus' Galilean ministry. The site of some of His early miracles and of the calling of some of His disciples.

Christ. Greek for the Hebrew word *Messiah,* which means "Anointed One." Throughout the Old Testament God promised to send the Messiah to deliver His people from their enemies and to set up His kingdom. Jesus is that Messiah.

church. The collective gathering of God's people. The New Testament speaks of the church both as the Christians gathered in a specific place and as all Christians everywhere of all time. It is also described as the fellowship of God's people, the bride of Christ, the body of Christ, and a building of which Jesus Christ is the chief cornerstone.

circumcision. Removal of the foreskin of the penis. Circumcision was a stipulation of the covenant God made with Abraham and his descendants. It showed that He would be their God, and they were to belong to Him. Controversy erupted in the early Christian church about whether Gentile Christians needed to be circumcised. St. Paul spoke God's Word to this controversy when he declared that circumcision was not required of Gentiles who became Christians.

congregation. An assembly of people gathered for worship and religious instruction; a collective, religious group.

conversion. An act of God's grace by which a sinful person is turned around and brought into God's kingdom. Conversion is accomplished by the Holy Spirit, who brings the person to faith in Christ through the Word.

covenant. An agreement between two or more tribes, nations, or individuals in which one or all of the parties promise under oath to do or refrain from doing something. Scripture records a number of covenants God has made with His people.

deacon. Someone who serves. In the early church, deacons were chosen to relieve the apostles of caring for the physical needs of widows and other poor people.

demons. Evil spirits who are against God and His work. They are angels who rebelled against God and now follow Satan.

disciples. Students or learners. In the New Testament disciples most often refers to Jesus' followers. Sometimes it refers specifically to the Twelve, but often it applies to a larger group of those who followed Jesus and learned from His teaching. *See also* apostles.

doctrine. Instruction or teaching; a body of beliefs about such theological issues as God, Christ, humanity, the church, and salvation.

Easter. Originally a pagan festival honoring a Teutonic (ancient Germanic) goddess of light and spring. By the eighth century the name was applied to the commemoration of Christ's resurrection.

elder. In the New Testament, *elder* and *bishop* are both used to mean "oversees." The elder or presbyter was a man the apostles appointed in each Christian congregation to be its spiritual leader.

elect. The elect are those who have faith in Christ as the promised Messiah and Savior.

election. The doctrine that explains the biblical truth that God from eternity planned our salvation and chose by His grace those who will be saved in Christ. No one deserves to be saved. God, however, desires that all people be saved. By God's grace through faith alone in Jesus, people (the elect) are saved. Those who have received God's gift of faith respond in thankfulness to God for His love and grace in choosing them.

epistle. A formal letter; one of the letters adopted as books of the New Testament.

eternal life. Abiding fellowship with God of infinite duration. Eternal life begins when the Holy Spirit by grace brings a person to faith in Jesus Christ. Although the Christian already has eternal life, he or she will not experience it fully until the resurrection of the dead and the life of the world to come.

faith. The belief and trust in the promise of God in Christ Jesus, worked by the Holy Spirit, through which a person is brought into a right relationship with God and saved. The Holy Spirit works faith in Christ in the individual through Word and Sacrament.

fellowship. Sharing something in common. By grace, through faith in Christ, God has given believers fellowship—that is, an intimate relationship—with Himself. Through the work of the Holy Spirit, fellow believers also have a oneness in Christ and share with one another the common bond of the Gospel and faith in Christ.

forgiveness. God's act whereby He ends the separation caused by peoples' sins and restores people to a proper relationship with Him. Forgiveness is a gift of God, given out of grace for Christ's sake. As a result of Christ's forgiveness, we are to forgive our neighbor. Recognizing that we are sinful and being sorry for our sins precedes forgiveness.

Gentiles. Non-Hebrew peoples of the world; people outside the Jewish faith.

glory. That which shows the greatness of someone or something. The glory of God is shown in and by His great miracles, His eternal perfection, His creation, and all His works. Most important, it is shown by His Son, our Lord Jesus Christ, and the salvation He won for all people.

Gnosticism. A belief system that reached its peak in the second and third centuries A.D. According to the Gnostics, salvation came by hating the world and everything physical and by escaping to the spirit world through special knowledge. Gnostics said Jesus came not to save people from sin but to show them how to escape to the spiritual world.

Gospel (Good News). The message that Jesus Christ has fulfilled the Law for all people and paid the penalty for their sin on the cross, thus having won forgiveness and salvation for them.

gospels. The first four books of the New Testament. Matthew, Mark, Luke, and John each wrote one of the books. They are called gospels because they tell the good news of how salvation was won for all people by Jesus Christ.

grace. God's undeserved love and favor revealed in Jesus Christ by which He is moved to forgive people's sins and grant them salvation. The word *grace* is sometimes used to mean a gift, quality, or virtue. Saving grace, however, is none of these things. It is a quality within God. It is also referred to as God's steadfast love or faithfulness.

heaven. The invisible world or universe from which God rules; the home of angels. Christ rules from heaven and receives believers there. *See also* paradise.

heir. The individual to whom another person's wealth or possessions—the person's inheritance—is given after the person dies.

hell. The place of eternal punishment or the punishment itself.

heresy. Stubborn error in an article of faith in opposition to Scripture.

holy. Without sin; an essential aspect of God's nature. Those who trust in Christ for salvation have been declared holy and righteous in God's sight. The Holy Spirit, through the Gospel, works in believers to motivate and empower them to lead lives of holiness. *Holy* can also be used to refer to something set apart to be used for or by God.

hymn. A song telling about God and praising Him.

inspiration. The special way the Holy Spirit worked in certain people to cause them to act out, speak, or write God's Word. When the Holy Spirit did this, the person who was inspired was certainly under the direction of God's power, but he or she was not a robot. As Paul says, "All Scripture is God-breathed" (2 Timothy 3:16).

Israel. (1) The name given to Jacob after he wrestled with God (Genesis 32:28). (2) The name of the nation composed of the descendants of Jacob and his 12 sons. Jacob and his sons founded the 12 tribes of Israel. (3) The name given to the 10 northern tribes of Israel after Solomon's death, when they revolted against Rehoboam and the kingdom split in two. The Northern Kingdom was called Israel to distinguish it from the Southern Kingdom, which was called Judah. (4) All who follow in the faith of Abraham, Isaac, and Jacob and therefore are true Israelites, no matter what their physical descent.

Jerusalem. The state and religious capital of the Hebrew nation. Jesus was arrested, tried, and crucified in Jerusalem.

Jesus. Greek for the Hebrew name *Joshua,* which means "Yahweh (the LORD) saves."

Jew. A later derivation of the word *Judean,* which referred to someone who belonged to the tribe or kingdom of Judah (Southern Kingdom) as opposed to the Northern Kingdom. *Hebrew* denotes those who descended from Abraham through Isaac and Jacob; *Israel* denotes those who descended from Jacob; and *Judean,* later *Jew,* denotes those who descended from the tribe or kingdom of Judah. As well as being an ethnic designation, the term *Jew* also refers to the adherents of a religion. While in New Testament times some Jews were faithful adherents of the faith of the Old Testament, others had begun to deviate from that faith. During the time between the Old and New Testaments, a number of Jewish religious groups had developed, such as the Pharisees and the Sadducees. The pharisaic branch survived after New Testament times and has most influenced the religion called Judaism, which is composed of a combination of oral tradition and Old Testament beliefs. *See also* Pharisees.

Jordan River. The river that connects the Sea of Galilee to the Dead Sea. It is the river in which Jesus was baptized by John.

Judah. (1) The fourth son of Jacob and Leah. Jacob bestowed the blessing of the birthright on Judah. Jesus was one of Judah's descendants. (2) The tribe that descended from Judah. It occupied the greater part of southern Palestine. (3) The kingdom of Judah, which began when the 10 northern tribes withdrew from Rehoboam around 930 B.C. The kingdom of Judah, which occupied the southern part of Palestine, lasted until 587 B.C., when Jerusalem fell to the Babylonians.

justification. The gracious act of God by which He pronounces people to be not guilty of their sin through faith in Jesus. The basis for His acquittal is that Jesus Christ fulfilled the Law in humanity's place and paid the penalty for all people's sin by His suffering and death on the cross.

kingdom of God. A spiritual kingdom, ruled by God, that includes people from all nations. The New Testament sometimes pictures God's kingdom as the rule of the Holy Spirit in the hearts of God's people. The kingdom of God is, at times, spoken of as a future blessing, as in the kingdom Jesus will bring on the Last Day, and, at times, described as a present reality. The church proclaims the kingdom of God by preaching the Gospel.

Lord. (1) LORD (printed in capital and small capital letters) is the way *Yahweh*, God's personal name in the Old Testament, is often rendered in English. (2) Lord (capital *L* and the remaining letters lowercase) comes from the Hebrew word *adon*. It means "master" and denotes ownership. (3) At some point, probably after the exile, God's people stopped pronouncing *Yahweh* and instead said *Adonai* whenever they saw the consonants for *Yahweh* (YHWH) in the Hebrew Bible. (4) The Greek word *kyrios* is also translated as Lord. It is the word used for a human master or for God as ruler, and is also used to refer to Christ.

Lord's Supper. Christ instituted this supper on the night of His betrayal. It is to be celebrated in the church until His return as a proclamation of His death for the sins of the world. In this meal, Christ gives His body and blood in, with, and under the bread and wine. Christians who trust in the blessings Christ promises to give in this meal and who partake of it in faith receive through it forgiveness of sins, life, salvation, and a strengthening of their faith. Also called "Breaking of Bread," "Holy Communion," "Eucharist," and "the Lord's Table."

love. Various types of love are referred to in the Bible. The Greek word *agape* represents God's sacrificial and intentional love for sinful people. This is the kind of love Christians are to have.

mercy. The aspect of God's character that moves Him to spare us from hurtful things even though we deserve them and to help those in distress. As Christians have been shown mercy by God, they are to be merciful to others.

Messiah. Hebrew for "Anointed One." *See also* Christ.

minister. A person who has been called—by God, through the church—to spiritually feed and care for God's people. All Christians have vocations—callings by God in life. All Christians have received various gifts of the Holy Spirit for the building up of others in the church. All Christians are members of the priesthood of all believers (1 Peter 2:9). However, just as Jesus chose 12 of His disciples to serve as apostles, God distinctly calls some people to be minister.

miracle. An event that causes wonder; something that takes place outside of the laws of nature. The New Testament depicts miracles as signs, wonders, and acts of power. Their significance could be understood only by those who had faith in Jesus Christ.

Nazareth. Jesus' hometown. The place where He grew up after His family returned from Egypt. Jesus was not well received in Nazareth when He returned during His ministry.

ordination. A rite (act) of the church by which the church through a congregation publicly confers the pastoral office on a qualified man. Ordination has its historical roots in the New Testament and in the early church. In the New Testament, deacons, missionaries, and elders were called to their offices, just as today a congregation calls a man to be its pastor.

parable. An earthly story with a heavenly or spiritual meaning: a saying or story that uses an illustration from everyday life for the purpose of teaching a moral or religious truth. Although the events and characters in the parable are true to nature, not every detail of the story has a spiritual meaning. Rather, there is only one main point of comparison. Jesus often spoke in parables to teach the people about Himself and the kingdom of heaven.

paradise. Used in the New Testament to describe heaven, the home of those who die in Christ. *See also* heaven.

peace. Often used to describe that state of spiritual tranquility and harmony that God gives when He brings one into a right relationship with Himself.

Pentecost. The Jewish Feast of Weeks, which was celebrated 50 days after the offering of the barley sheaf during the Feast of Unleavened Bread. Pentecost is also known as the Feast of Harvest and the Day of Firstfruits. On this day the Holy Spirit was poured out on the disciples, and many people came to faith in Christ after hearing Peter's Spirit-filled preaching.

Pharisees. One of several Jewish religious parties in New Testament times, primarily made up of people from the middle class. They were characterized by scrupulous keeping of the mosaic law and the oral traditions added to the Law. It was their desire to make the Law understandable and applicable so that people might fully obey it. Thus, they formulated lists of rules, spelling out exactly, for example, what constituted work on the Sabbath. In this way they sought to build a "fence" around the Law to keep people from getting close to violating its commandments. In general, the Jews highly respected the Pharisees. Some Pharisees, such as Nicodemus, were sincere in their beliefs, but many others fell into hypocrisy, living by the letter of the Law and not following its spirit.

prayer. Speaking with God. Prayers can be formal or spoken freely from one's own thoughts and concerns. They can be said together by a group of believers or alone by an individual. They can be said at set times and places or all times and places.

priests. One who represents the people before God. Through Moses, God appointed Aaron and his descendants as priests. They wore special clothing in the sanctuary, taught the people, and inquired of God's will. The chief priest, or high priest, was in charge of all other priests. He offered the sin offering, made sacrifice on the Day of Atonement, and discovered the will of God through Urim and Thummim. In the New Testament, Jesus Christ is the only high priest. Since He sacrificed Himself for the sins of the people and this sacrifice need never be repeated, there is no longer a need for the Levitical priesthood. The New Testament also teaches the priesthood of all believers. Christians share in Christ's priestly activity by bringing the Gospel to people.

Redeemer. The one who buys back. Jesus Christ. *See also* redemption.

redemption. The buying back of humanity from sin and death by Christ, the Redeemer, who paid the price with His perfect obedience and His sacrificial death on the cross.

repentance. A total change of heart and life that God works in an individual who does not believe or trust in Him by turning him or her around to believe and trust in Him. Repentance includes both sorrow for one's sins and faith in Christ through whom forgiveness is granted.

resurrection. A return to life after one has died.

righteous. That which is right in accordance with the Law. The term is particularly used to describe people who are in a right relationship with God through faith in Christ.

sacrament. A sacred act instituted by God where there are visible means connected to His Word. In a sacrament God offers, gives, and seals to the individual the forgiveness of sins earned by Christ.

sacrifice. An act of worship where a person presents an offering to God. God commanded sacrifices in the Old Testament as a way for sins to be atoned for and as a means for people to express thankfulness to Him. Among the main sacrifices mentioned in the Old Testament are the sin offering, the trespass offering, the burnt offering, the peace offering, and the meal and drink offerings. Among other times, offerings were sacrificed on the altar on the morning and evening, at each Sabbath and new moon, and at the three leading festivals. All sacrifices pointed to and were fulfilled in Christ, the Lamb of God, who was sacrificed for the sins of the world.

salvation. Deliverance from any type of evil, both physical and spiritual. Spiritual salvation includes rescue from sin. It is a gift of God's grace through faith in Christ.

Samaria. During Old Testament times, the capital city of the Northern Kingdom of Israel. During New Testament times, the land of the Samaritans between Galilee in the north and Judea in the south. Interestingly, the most direct route from Nazareth to Jerusalem led directly through Samaria; however, most Jews would avoid that route, taking a significant detour across the Jordan River and then south.

Samaritans. A mixed race of people descended partly from the tribes of the Northern Kingdom of Israel and partly from Gentiles settled in Israel during the exilic period of the Old Testament. The Samaritans worshiped the God of Israel, but their religion differed from that of the Jews in significant ways. For example, Samaritans accepted the authority of the Pentateuch only and rejected the rest of the Hebrew scriptures. Jews and Samaritans, although culturally very similar, lived on "opposite sides of the tracks." They were often bigoted toward each other and avoided each other. Jews thought that the Samaritans, like tax collectors, had no place in the messianic kingdom.

Satan. The chief fallen angel and enemy of God, humanity, and all that is good. Sometimes called Abaddon, Apollyon, or Beelzebul (Beelzebub).

Sea of Galilee. A body of water fed by the Jordan River. Jesus spent much of His early ministry around the Sea of Galilee. The sea is the place where Jesus walked on water and calmed the storm. During New Testament times, the sea (more properly considered a lake) supported a large fishing industry.

sin. Both doing what God forbids and failing to do what He commands. Because of sin everyone deserves temporal and eternal death. Only through faith in Christ, who kept God's Law perfectly and suffered the punishment for the sins of the world, does one escape the results of sin.

Son of God. A title applied to Jesus in a unique sense. It says that Jesus as the Son is equal to God the Father.

Son of Man. The term Jesus most often used to refer to Himself. This title emphasizes the power and dominion Jesus receives from the Ancient of Days. (See Daniel 7:9, 13–14 and Matthew 16:27.)

soul, spirit. The immaterial essence that animates the flesh. The soul (often called the spirit) is not separate from the body; rather it is that which gives life. It is the inner person as distinguished from the flesh. It is the seat of the appetites, emotions, and passions. The soul departs at death. It can be lost and saved.

Suffering Servant. A synonym for Jesus. Jesus is the fulfillment of the Suffering Servant prophesied in the Old Testament (Isaiah 42:1–4; 49:1–6; 50:4–9; 52:13–53:12).

tabernacle. The movable tent that God commanded His people to build after He delivered them from bondage in Egypt. God promised to dwell among His people in the tabernacle (Exodus 25:8). The tabernacle served as Israel's center of worship until Solomon's temple was built. *See also* temple.

tax collectors. In New Testament times, the people who collected taxes for the Roman Empire. Roman taxes were very high, and it was the practice of the empire to hand over the collection of taxes to individuals or businesses, who would add a certain percentage to the amount collected. Needless to say, this system, called "tax farming," was open to abuse. Most Jews hated tax collectors, viewing them as usurers and thieves who supported the godless Roman oppressors. Tax collectors were deemed unclean. They were cut off from the people of God and were thought to have no place in the messianic kingdom.

teachers of the law. Specialists in and teachers of Jewish ceremonial, civil, and moral laws.

temple. The fixed sanctuary of the Lord that replaced the tabernacle as God's dwelling place among His people. The temple was the center of Israelite and then Jewish worship until it was destroyed. Jesus, God who took on human flesh, replaced the temple as God's dwelling place among His people (John 1:14; John 2:19–21; Revelation 21:22). *See also* tabernacle.

testament. A document outlining the distribution of a person's property after death. When the Old Testament (originally written in Hebrew and Aramaic) was translated into Greek, the Hebrew word for "covenant" was translated with the Greek word for "testament." This same Greek word is used in Jesus' Words of Institution (see Mark 14:24) and is translated by some as covenant and by others as testament. *See also* covenant.

tithe. A tenth part of one's income given as an offering to the Lord. According to the Law, a tenth of all produce of land and herds was sacred to the Lord.

transfiguration. The name given to the occasion when Jesus was visibly glorified in the presence of three of His disciples.

Trinity. The church's term for the coexistence of Father, Son, and Holy Spirit in the unity of the Godhead—three distinct persons in one divine being, or essence. The term *Trinity* does not occur in the Bible, but many passages support the doctrine of the Trinity.

unleavened bread. Bread made without yeast. The Israelites ate unleavened bread at Passover and the subsequent Feast of Unleavened Bread as a reminder of the haste with which they left Egypt during the exodus. During the exodus, they did not have time to bake bread but took with them unleavened dough that they baked in the wilderness.

will. Inclination or choice. God's will is revealed in His acts, His Law, and especially in Christ. Although the will of fallen human beings has some capacity to perform works that conform outwardly to God's Law, humanity's fallen or natural will cannot incline itself toward God or choose to have true faith in Him. Only the Holy Spirit working through the Gospel can create in people true faith in God, thereby inclining a person's will to good. *See also* works.

Word. God's Word is the means through which He makes Himself known and reveals His will to humanity. His Word is the primary way through which He works His purposes in the world. The Holy Scriptures are the written Word of God. They tell of the purpose of God in creating, saving, and sanctifying His people. They testify to Jesus Christ, the Word of God made flesh. Jesus Christ is the supreme revelation of God. He is the living Word.

works. Deeds. Whether a person's works are ultimately deemed good or bad in God's sight depends on that person's relationship to God. Only a person who believes in Jesus Christ as Savior can do good works in God's eyes, since good works are a fruit of faith.

world. Used in Scripture not only to describe the universe or the human race, but often to denote the wicked and the unbelieving, that is, those who are opposed to God.

worship. To bow down, kiss the hand, revere, or serve. The respect and reverence given to God. New Testament worship is centered in and around the Word of God. It involves reading Scripture, singing hymns and spiritual songs, teaching, praying, and celebrating the Lord's Supper. In Christian worship, God bestows His gifts of forgiveness, life, and salvation upon us through His Word and Sacraments, and we respond in thankfulness and praise.

Zealots. Members of an ultra nationalistic first-century A.D. Jewish political group. They were similar to the Pharisees in their general beliefs, but where the Pharisees might be ready to die for their faith, the Zealots were ready to kill for it. They advocated the use of force against the Romans.